Norfolk from the Air
Volume 2

Norfolk from the Air

Volume 2

Photography principally by
Derek Edwards

Edited by
Peter Wade-Martins

Assistant Editor
Jane Everett

Archaeology & Environment Division
Norfolk Museums Service

© Copyright Norfolk Museums Service 1999

ISBN 0 903101 68 8

1st Edition 1999

Designed by Dick Malt

Printed by Witley Press Ltd
Hunstanton, Norfolk

Typeset in Eras and Rotis Serif

The illustrations on the half-title and title pages are details of numbers 8 and 68 respectively.

Contents

Introduction page 7
Map of sites page 8
Acknowledgements page 144
Dates and sources of the photographs page 145
Suggestions for further reading page 146
Index of place names page 147

Illustrations

Introduction **1**
Coastal scenes **2-11** 
Landscapes **12-17** 
Neolithic and Bronze Age **18-25** 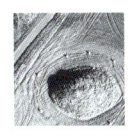
Iron Age **26-28** 
Roman **29-38** 
Medieval monasteries **45-52**  
Medieval castles **39-44**
Medieval churches **53-56**
Medieval countryside **57-66** 
Great houses **67-78** 
The farming scene **79-86** 
Villages **87-88**  
Norwich **101-111**
Market towns **89-100**
Industry **112-114**
The Broads **115-123**
Norwich southern bypass **124-125** 
Military installations **126-128** 
New impacts on the landscape **129-134** 
The North Sea **135**

Frontispiece
Thurne

TG 400 157 Open

The River Thurne, busy with holiday traffic, flows past Thurne village seen here at the head of its dyke. The two mills are in fact windpumps, built to drain the adjacent marshes into the river. The nearer, with its four-storey brick tower, is St Benet's Level pump, dating from the late eighteenth century and restored in 1976. The other is Thurne Mill, built in 1820, restored 1949-55 and fitted with new sails in 1962.

Introduction

Norfolk from the Air was originally published in 1987 with photographs illustrating a wide range of historic landscapes from the Stone Age to the twentieth century. This gave readers an insight into the landscape which is seldom apparent at ground level, and also made the point quite successfully that features such as long barrows and railway stations are all part of the same story of continuous change. Most landscape features in Norfolk, as elsewhere, become obsolete with time. Few remain unaltered for long.

Demand for the book was such that it was reprinted after only eight weeks, but it nevertheless was soon out of print again, and so it remained for several years, rapidly achieving a rarity value. Ten years later it was re-published, without the colour section, as volume I of this new two-part work.

This volume, part II of the set, retains the best of the original colour photography, and offers much more colour, together with a wide selection of new black-and-white material. We hope that it will provide as much pleasure and interest as the first clearly did.

Forty-nine specialists have kindly contributed captions to the photographs in this volume. It starts with coastal scenes and characteristic Norfolk landscapes. Thereafter, there is a chronological sequence illustrating prehistoric monuments, historic landscapes and modern features. They are all part of the same evolving story. The view of the now-demolished power station at Yarmouth (114) and the picture of the Roman settlement at Hockwold, where even the post-holes of some of the timber buildings are visible as marks in the growing corn (31), are both important in the archaeological record.

It is interesting that some monuments, whilst separated in time by several thousand years, can leave superficially similar traces. Compare, for instance, the shape and form of the imprint left by the ring-ditch of a Bronze Age burial mound (24), Iron Age round-houses (28), and a Second World War searchlight battery (127). Aerial photography can still teach us much about our past, and it has proved to be an invaluable method of research and of recording our changing landsape.

Over the intervening years, since the first publication of Norfolk from the Air in 1987, many remarkable sites have been recorded. The discovery of the Roman forts at Saham Toney (32/33) and Swanton Morley (34), and the outline of a long-demolished church at East Rudham (51) emphasise the incompleteness of our present knowledge, and the need for continued aerial survey and photography. There is still so much more to discover.

Most of the photographs in these companion volumes have been taken by Derek Edwards over the last twenty-five years as part of the air photography programme of the Field Archaeology Division of Norfolk Museums Service.

The Norfolk Air Photographs Library, held at Gressenhall, is probably the largest county-based archive of its type in Britain. The collection includes copies of rare photographs taken by the Royal Flying Corps on training missions from 1917, complete coverage of the county by the Royal Air Force National Air Survey of 1946, the Royal Air Force 'Floodlight Project' photography of the east-coast floods of February 1953, a full-colour vertical aerial survey by the National Remote Sensing Centre from December 1994 to May 1995, and historic oblique aerial photography taken by George Swain (1921-1974) and H. Frederick Low (1932-1954). This complements the work of the Field Archaeology Division from 1974 to the present day.

Altogether, the Air Photographs Library offers a remarkable record of Norfolk in the twentieth century and we are delighted to be able to bring another fascinating selection to the notice of a wider public.

Picture location and orientation

Accompanying the picture titles is the grid reference indicating approximately the centre point of each picture. Guidance for the use of the grid reference system is given on Ordnance Survey maps. Comparison of the aerial photographs with OS maps will often assist the reader, and a north pointer is provided after the caption to help with orientation.

Note on access to sites

Many of the sites illustrated in this book are on private property and are not open to the public. Sites or areas which are open regularly to visitors are marked by the word 'open' in the title panel beneath each picture.

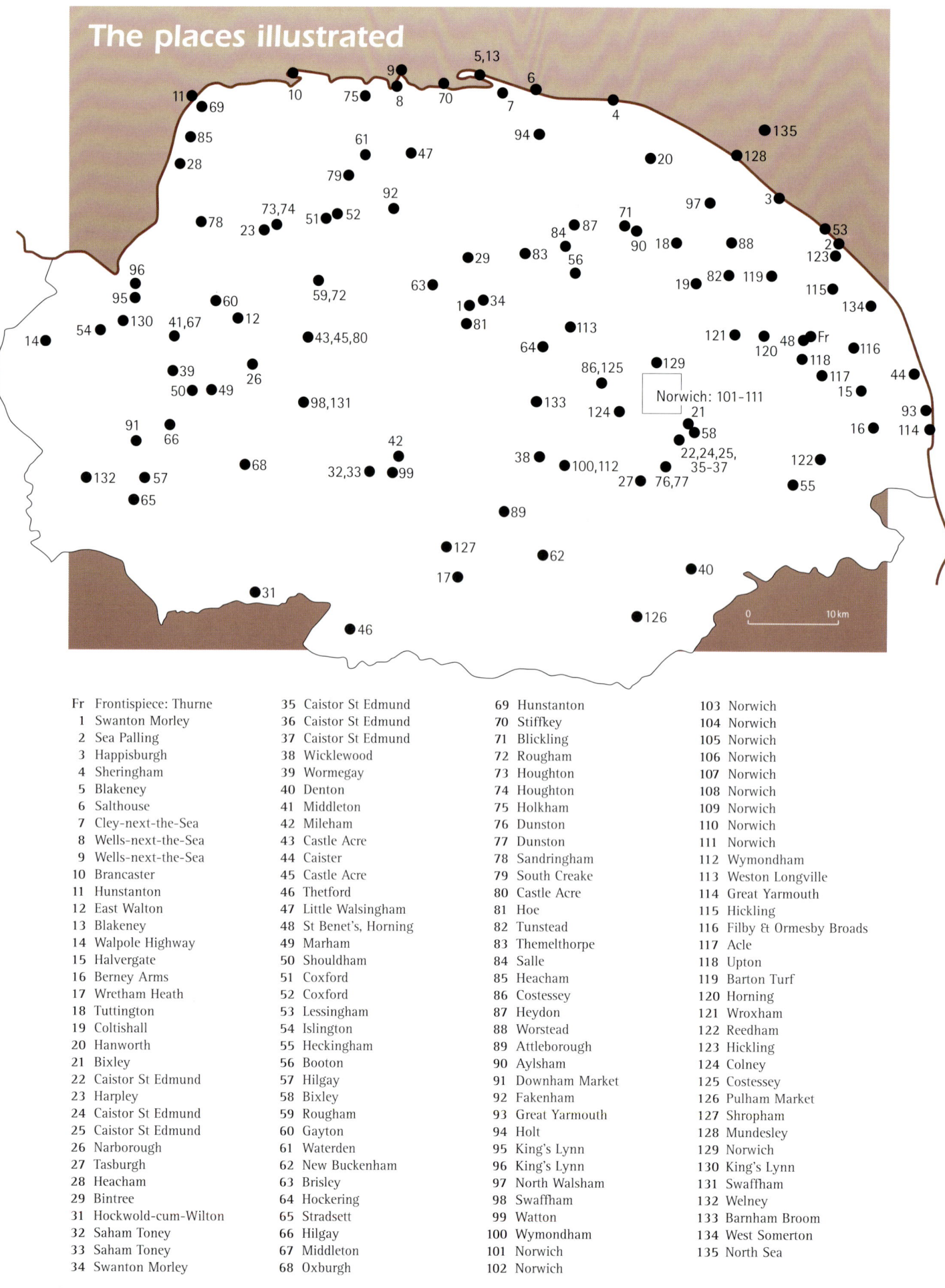

The places illustrated

Fr	Frontispiece: Thurne	35 Caistor St Edmund	69 Hunstanton	103 Norwich
1	Swanton Morley	36 Caistor St Edmund	70 Stiffkey	104 Norwich
2	Sea Palling	37 Caistor St Edmund	71 Blickling	105 Norwich
3	Happisburgh	38 Wicklewood	72 Rougham	106 Norwich
4	Sheringham	39 Wormegay	73 Houghton	107 Norwich
5	Blakeney	40 Denton	74 Houghton	108 Norwich
6	Salthouse	41 Middleton	75 Holkham	109 Norwich
7	Cley-next-the-Sea	42 Mileham	76 Dunston	110 Norwich
8	Wells-next-the-Sea	43 Castle Acre	77 Dunston	111 Norwich
9	Wells-next-the-Sea	44 Caister	78 Sandringham	112 Wymondham
10	Brancaster	45 Castle Acre	79 South Creake	113 Weston Longville
11	Hunstanton	46 Thetford	80 Castle Acre	114 Great Yarmouth
12	East Walton	47 Little Walsingham	81 Hoe	115 Hickling
13	Blakeney	48 St Benet's, Horning	82 Tunstead	116 Filby & Ormesby Broads
14	Walpole Highway	49 Marham	83 Themelthorpe	117 Acle
15	Halvergate	50 Shouldham	84 Salle	118 Upton
16	Berney Arms	51 Coxford	85 Heacham	119 Barton Turf
17	Wretham Heath	52 Coxford	86 Costessey	120 Horning
18	Tuttington	53 Lessingham	87 Heydon	121 Wroxham
19	Coltishall	54 Islington	88 Worstead	122 Reedham
20	Hanworth	55 Heckingham	89 Attleborough	123 Hickling
21	Bixley	56 Booton	90 Aylsham	124 Colney
22	Caistor St Edmund	57 Hilgay	91 Downham Market	125 Costessey
23	Harpley	58 Bixley	92 Fakenham	126 Pulham Market
24	Caistor St Edmund	59 Rougham	93 Great Yarmouth	127 Shropham
25	Caistor St Edmund	60 Gayton	94 Holt	128 Mundesley
26	Narborough	61 Waterden	95 King's Lynn	129 Norwich
27	Tasburgh	62 New Buckenham	96 King's Lynn	130 King's Lynn
28	Heacham	63 Brisley	97 North Walsham	131 Swaffham
29	Bintree	64 Hockering	98 Swaffham	132 Welney
31	Hockwold-cum-Wilton	65 Stradsett	99 Watton	133 Barnham Broom
32	Saham Toney	66 Hilgay	100 Wymondham	134 West Somerton
33	Saham Toney	67 Middleton	101 Norwich	135 North Sea
34	Swanton Morley	68 Oxburgh	102 Norwich	

Derek Edwards, Aerial Photography Officer

Introduction 1

Since 1973, Derek Edwards, as Aerial Photography Officer for the Field Archaeology Division of Norfolk Museums Service, has been regularly flying the county recording sites and landscapes in all weathers and at all times of the year. His flight records show that over this period he has spent 672 hours in the air, taking 41,000 photographs. His aerial survey work has revealed hundreds of important archaeological sites not previously recorded. His photographs now form the core of the Norfolk Aerial Photographs Library.

A member of the Council for British Archaeology Aerial Archaeology Research Committee from 1976 to 1991, Derek Edwards is currently President of NAPLIB (the National Association of Aerial Photographic Libraries) and editor of the journal *Aerial Archaeology*. Since 1973, some 1500 of his photographs have been published in academic journals, books of local and national interest, and the news media.

The Cessna 150 aircraft - the ubiquitous American 'car of the air' - has proved to be an ideal machine for aerial photography. Readily available from local flying schools and Aero Clubs at reasonable cost, the high-wing profile, combined with good handling characteristics and relatively low air-speed, make it an ideal platform for aerial photography.

Coastal scenes

2 Sea Palling offshore sea defences

TG 425 284 Open

This photograph epitomises the efforts made to prevent the sea flooding parts of East Anglia. The photographer's plane was just off the lifeboat house at Sea Palling, and this north-westward view extends almost to North Gap at Eccles. On the left are the outlying summer cottages nestling behind the dunes at the northern end of Sea Palling. The narrow line of dunes along this coast is occasionally breached, as in 1938 (at Horsey) and in 1953 (at Sea Palling). After 1953 a concrete wall was built in front of the dunes, but in recent years low beach levels have exposed the base of the wall and made it liable to collapse in winter storms. The low beaches have in part been caused by effective defence of the eroding cliffs further north which supply sand to the beaches to the south. To prevent further breaches (and the incursion of salt water into the northern part of the Broads) large rocks have been placed against the foot of the sea wall and after that, as an even more effective defence, offshore reefs have been built from huge Scandinavian boulders. These cut off the wave energy that can reach the beach, so reducing the effectiveness of the wave-powered longshore drift that moves sand on the beach towards the south. This allows sand to accumulate in the quieter water in the lee of each reef, producing the incipient nesses and bays seen here. Since this photo was taken, sand has been fed to the beach from offshore and the beach has built out, almost reaching the northernmost reef, and has built up high enough against the wall to completely cover the rocks so obvious here.

Cliff erosion at Happisburgh

Coastal scenes

3

TG 386 308 Open

Taken on the same wild day as the picture of the floods at Salthouse (6), this picture shows the North Sea pounding the cliffs at Happisburgh. The village lies almost at the southern end of the Norfolk cliffs, and in the past, sand eroded from the high cliffs between here and Cromer was moved by the sea to this site in sufficient volume to maintain a wide beach. Wave attack on the cliffs was limited, so that the rate of erosion was only about one third of a metre a year. This, and an absence of planning control before 1947, encouraged the building of holiday homes on the cliff-top in the interwar years. These houses in turn encouraged the local Rural District Council to construct revetments and groynes after the 1953 surge to try to further reduce wave attack on the cliffs. For many reasons these measures were only effective for a decade or two and as, beach levels have fallen, the cliffs have been eroding more rapidly. The defences themselves are collapsing now. Several houses at the southern end of Beach Road have been lost over the cliff edge and others will surely follow. North of the lifeboat station, mobile caravans represent a better adjustment to providing accommodation close to the sea on an eroding coastline.

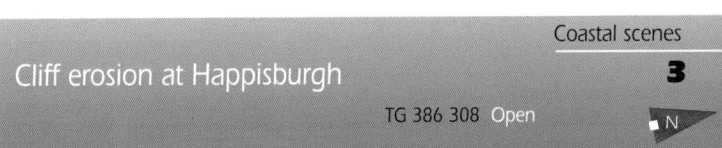

It is hard to justify the high expenditure required for coastal defences when most of the cliff-top is fields, so it may be that this part of the coast will be left to erode naturally. If so, the beach will build up as the cliff moves inland and eventually the rate of erosion will reduce to its natural level.

Coastal scenes

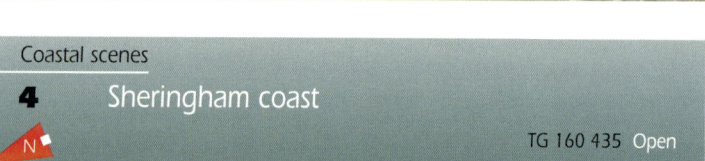

4 Sheringham coast

TG 160 435 Open

This superb view of the curve of the Norfolk coast from Sheringham (in the foreground) round to Cromer and beyond shows the two towns (Cromer can be located by the pier, the dark tower of the church and the white lighthouse to the right of that), the villages and countryside between and the wooded slopes of the Cromer Ridge on the right. The railway into Sheringham and the golf course above the high cliffs in the foreground are other significant features. The varied adjustments made on an eroding cliffed coastline are seen; the towns tend to stand forward, protected by their sea walls, while the wide bays between mark lengths less vigorously defended because less built property is at risk. In particular, the impressive sea walls at Sheringham stand out with dark shadows on this north-ward-facing coast. The long-term rate of erosion here is not particularly high - about half a metre a year is typical - so it has taken many decades for these contrasts to develop. The golf course, as 'rural' land, is undefended, and already some of the greens have been moved as the cliff top works slowly landward.

As is typical of the British coast, groynes have been built as part of the coastal defences to try and increase beach width, and even the rural coast between Sheringham and West Runton is currently protected by a wooden revetment parallel to the shore with groynes on its seaward side. The sharp edge of Sheringham itself is a result of our national planning policies confining development to areas within a boundary drawn on a map, no doubt reinforced, as in the case of the golf course, by patterns of land ownership.

Blakeney	Coastal scenes
TG 027 441 Open	5

During the Middle Ages, Blakeney held a fish fair as famous as that of Yarmouth. There, merchants from London and the Royal Household bought large quantities of salt fish. But whereas Yarmouth specialised in herring, Blakeney was the centre for cod and ling.

Mariner's Hill, seen behind the left of the quay, was used as a lookout for ships approaching Blakeney. Although trade had largely declined, villagers still greatly objected in 1900 to the quarrying of the hill for road building. To the right of Mariner's Hill are the remains of the incorrectly titled Guildhall, which was more probably the fourteenth-century undercroft of a merchant's house. To the left, the land used to belong to the Carmelite Friary, founded in 1296. The old commercial centre may well have been directly in front of the church (top left) on land marked on an eighteenth-century map as 'church green, formerly the market place'. The eastern turret of Blakeney church was used as a lighthouse for shipping, but was probably of more navigational use during daylight, helping to distinguish Blakeney from other churches when viewed from the sea.

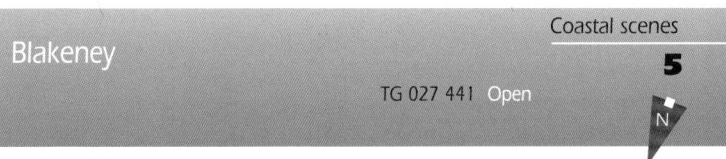

The road to Holt, formerly the Holgate Way, can be seen centre top. Running parallel, to the left, the field boundary marks the course of a former road to Cley, following the parish boundary.

In 1817 the Blakeney Harbour Company was formed and obtained permission to straighten and deepen the channel so that ships of 150 tons could use it. The *Taffy*, (173 tons) was reputedly the largest vessel to reach the quay; however, lighters were used to unload larger ships that would anchor in the deeper water behind Blakeney Point.

Coastal scenes

6 Salthouse after the 1996 storm

TG 081 440 Open

This view was taken on 21st February 1996, after a northerly storm and surge had flooded parts of the north Norfolk coast and a dusting of windblown snow had decorated the brown winter landscape. The fine shingle beach in the foreground continues out to Blakeney Point, marked by the distant curve of the breaking waves. When strong northerly winds blow south down the North Sea the water builds up to as much as 2m above the normal level (called a storm surge), and the combination of exceptionally high water levels and high waves can cause very serious flooding, as in 1938 and 1953. The 1996 event was more localised, but at Salthouse the shingle barrier was overtopped, washing shingle in a fan over the marsh and flooding the area behind the barrier, including the coast road and the houses and gardens along it at Salthouse itself (the village in the middle of the picture).

The straight bank running northward from Cley to the coast is designed to keep salt water out of this area which consists of reclaimed salt marsh managed as grazing land and a bird reserve. On this occasion the bank is delaying the escape of the floodwater and though the salt marshes to the west have shed their water as the surge has passed, the protected freshwater marsh remains flooded until the water can drain away via the sluices through the bank. It will be seen that the shingle bank has a steep crest, broken where the washover fans occur. This is a flood protection feature built by bulldozers each winter since 1953, but not always effective, as this photograph shows.

Cley-next-the-Sea

Coastal scenes

7

TG 045 440 Open

The sinuous course of the River Glaven, barely visible in front of the mill, bears little relation to the appearance it would have had in the sixteenth century when the busy port of Cley-next-the-Sea was sending ships as far away as Iceland and Crete. Even by the early years of the nineteenth century it was wide enough for the *Bell*, a vessel of 54ft (16.5m) in length, to be swung round at Cley Quay.

The change has largely been due to the reclamation of the salt marshes behind banks such as the one visible in the foreground (**Vol.1: 89**). Previous to the piecemeal embankment, the whole estuary as far inland as Glandford, as well as the marshes to the north-east (top left in the photograph) would have flooded during high spring tides. It was the scouring power of this water, ebbing from the marshland, which kept the channels free from silt. At low tide the Glaven split into two channels at the change in angle of the sea wall in front of the present terrace, known as Beau Rivage. One channel, known as *Milsteade*, followed the present course of the Glaven, whilst the other, called *Holfleete*, hugged the sea wall and buildings, before they both rejoined further inland near the church. In addition, a broad channel on the landward side of the shingle spit (top left) led to Salthouse.

The imposing, tall, white-fronted building to the right of the mill was the Customs House (built *c.*1680), an elegant reminder of the maritime prosperity of Cley before the port became a victim, first of the embanking, and later of competition from the railways.

Coastal scenes

8 Wells-next-the-Sea quay

▪▶ N   TF 917 438   Open

The contrast between settlements on the upland and the ever-changing patterns of the creeks and salt marshes is the great attraction of the north Norfolk coast. Wells is the only settlement still to have sea-going ships calling at it on the whole stretch of coast between King's Lynn and Great Yarmouth.

Wells is a tidal creek, not a river mouth, and it has undergone many alterations to give a maximum tidal scour along the channel. The sea bank built in 1859 deflects the channel seawards as well as protecting the Holkham marshes from flooding.

The photograph shows the seaward (northern) end of the town with its series of lanes which reach down to the quay. These are part of a grid pattern of streets of unknown date, although the market existed in 1202. A series of maltings marks the end of these lanes, reflecting the corn-growing hinterland of Wells, which has produced barley for centuries and from which barley, malt and wool were exported to London and Europe. Many of these maltings have now been converted into various facets of the tourist trade which now flourishes in Wells.

The earlier core of Wells lay to the south, off the picture, near to the large parish church of St Nicholas (patron saint of seafarers). A tidal channel once reached the toe of the upland on which the church lies and provided better shelter than the present quay. Sir Charles Turner of Warham built a sea wall to cut off this channel in 1719 and later still its other arm to Warham. To the west of Wells, in the background, lies the Holkham estate of the Earls of Leicester. Seaward of the coast road are reclaimed grazing marshes, protected by pine-covered sand dunes just off the photograph to the north.

Wells-next-the-Sea harbour entrance

Coastal scenes 9

TF 923 465 Open

This picture, taken from over West Sands, is looking eastwards along the eastern half of the low northern coastline of Norfolk. Fields and woods in the distance mark higher ground, in front of which are extensive salt marshes crossed by a complex network of channels which carry the tide and its load of mud in as the tide rises and drain out each time it falls. The seaward edge of the marshes has very wide sandy beaches, with dunes in the foreground planted in the nineteenth century with coniferous trees with the aim of increasing their stability. Some patches of dunes across the entrance to Wells Harbour (East Hills) are also tree-covered. Part of the reclaimed marsh behind the foreground dunes is occupied by a caravan camp, and the lifeboat station is on the point at the entrance to Wells Harbour.

The tide is close to the high tide mark for normal tides, for only Spring tides aided by storms fully cover the sandy beaches here; indeed, two patches of dunes which have grown over the last forty years can be seen in the foreground, the further one crowning the spit growing out in front of Wells Beach. A similar developing barrier is marked by the paler patches of sand east of the harbour entrance. The huge expanse of sand just submerged between this barrier and Blakeney Point (Bob Hall's Sands) is in turn fronted by a partially submerged barrier where the waves are breaking. This coastline is still building seawards as it accumulates sand from offshore and is illustrated in textbooks around the world as a classic example of a prograding barrier island coast.

Coastal scenes

10 Scolt Head, Brancaster

TF 793 460 Open

This picture looks eastward along the north Norfolk coast with Scolt Head Island in the foreground. The rising ground of the cultivated and wooded fields in the top right-hand corner of the photograph lies landward of an old sea cliff, long abandoned and so now sloping fairly gently up from the salt marshes and reclaimed meadows at its foot. On the shallow sea floor seaward of this old cliffline, beaches have built up facing the large waves which drive down the North Sea when the wind blows southward between Scotland and Norway. Close to these beaches of sand and shingle, sand dunes have added to this coastal barrier. In the sheltered shallow water behind, mud has accumulated and gradually built up to be colonised by such plants as samphire. The vegetation further quietens the water movement as the tides rise and fall, so encouraging even more rapid accumulation of mud to build salt marshes which now fill most of the space behind the outer barriers.

In the foreground the sand and shingle recurves at the west end of the island and the widening beach on the west side of the entrance to Brancaster harbour shows how dynamic this coastline is. Brancaster harbour entrance is to the right in the middle distance. The island is completed by the entrance to Burnham Overy Staithe in the distance, and beyond Holkham Bay is the entrance to Wells Harbour. The salt marshes depend on the water movement through these 'passes' in the outer barrier; over time they can shift along the coast as the spits extend - a process clearly seen at the eastern end of Scolt.

Hunstanton cliffs

Coastal scenes
11

TF 675 420 Open

This wide-ranging view covers the north-west corner of Norfolk, looking north east across Hunstanton from over the Wash. From just north of Hunstanton pier in the foreground to Gore Point at Holme next the Sea is 5km. From Gore Point along the north Norfolk coast to the western end of Scolt Head Island is another 8km, and the view continues in the distance to Holkham Bay. To the left, beyond St Edmund's Point, is Old Hunstanton. In the foreground is New Hunstanton, sensibly set back from the eroding cliff edge, and the wooded area behind the town is Hunstanton Park. The line of villages from Holme through Thornham (the white church tower) and Titchwell to Brancaster can be seen lying inland of the coastal marshes.

In the centre lie the large fields and scattered woodland belts so typical of this distinctive part of Norfolk which has the underlying chalk quite close to the surface. Whilst the northern coast and the broad bay between Gore and St Edmund's points have wide sandy beaches, local patches of sand dunes and extensive salt marshes (in places reclaimed for grazing), the coast in the foreground is formed by an impressive and nearly vertical cliff cut into the underlying geology by the waves. The foreshore and base of the cliffs expose the rusty brown carstone. The beds dip very gently downwards to the north, so the overlying chalk gradually drops down towards the beach from right to left. Here the basal bed of the chalk is a sandy limestone stained red or pink by iron oxides. Above it, the normal white chalk is a very pure limestone except where it includes nodules or layers of flint (**Vol.1: 3**).

Landscapes

12 East Walton pingos

TG 730 176

East Walton lies just over two miles north of Narborough and seven miles east south east of King's Lynn. This hummocky ground with rimmed ponds has survived for some 10,000 to 15,000 years because it is common land and consequently has not been cultivated - similar features can be seen as crop-marks in the foreground field, but they would be hard to interpret if we did not have for comparison the well-preserved pools and surrounding banks on the Common itself.

In this area, close to the Fenland margin, springs rise from the chalk which underlies the rising ground lying to the east and the water-table lies close to the surface. At the maximum of the last Ice Age, probably when Scottish ice reached as far south as the north Norfolk coast (about 18,000 years ago), the ground here was very deeply frozen all year, a condition known as permafrost.

Similar conditions may have returned about 10,000 years ago during another very cold period. The upwelling ground water could not escape through the frozen ground and formed huge mounds of ice covered by a layer of earth. Similar mounds occur today in the Mackenzie delta of Canada and are called by the eskimo word 'pingo'. Gradually as the cover of earth and soil thawed in the brief summers it slipped down to the base of the ice mound. The ice core melted as soon as the climate ameliorated, leaving a hollow surrounded by a low bank of earth rather like an irregular bomb crater.

Most of the pingos have been obliterated by cultivation, but they survive here and also at Thompson Common further south in Norfolk where there is a walk, with explanatory notices, known as the 'Pingo Trail'.

The road on the left is the main road east of Morston, with the outlying houses of Blakeney at the top of the picture. A curved section of the sea bank carrying the coastal path can just be seen in the top left-hand corner, with salt marsh to the left of it. Where it is not built over, the more gently sloping land here is in arable farming with large fields; a crop of potatoes is in the foreground.

The white gash is a gravel pit, cut into the northern end of an S-shaped ridge which is largely covered by heathland and scrub, reflecting steeper slopes and shallow soils over coarse gravel. Note the house on the crest in the middle foreground just above the first right-angled bend in the ridge, and another with a loop-shaped access track where the ridge twists southwards again to complete the 'S' shape. The ridge continues over Wiveton Down and almost to the Glaven valley at Glandford. The feature is known as the Blakeney esker: an esker is a ridge of gravel formed in a tunnel beneath a glacier or in a channel with ice on each side. Thus, this ridge dates back to a time when an ice sheet ended just south of the present coastline and meltwater escaped under pressure from beneath the ice. Its speed was high enough to carry the large cobbles which are characteristic of this ridge and the pressure carried it up over the ridge southwest of Wiveton at more than 30m above sea level. The outlying houses and bungalows of Blakeney are a reminder of the popularity of the North Norfolk coastal villages, especially for retirement.

Landscapes

The Blakeney esker

TG 017 436

Landscapes

14 Walpole Highway

TF 513 147

This is Marshland, the fertile siltlands lying between the Great Ouse and the Nene. 'Very flat!' Indeed, but there has been activity here since the Bronze Age, and it is a landscape well worth exploring. The slightly raised levees of former watercourses - roddons - snake across present-day fields; and nearer the coast stand the mounds associated with medieval saltmaking. Modern traffic flows through Marshland in roughly an east/west direction, from Lynn along the A17 to Sutton Bridge, and along the A47 to Wisbech. But look at the region's minor roads and you discover a predominantly north/south alignment. This is the ancient road system that allowed movement backwards and forwards in each parish between the main focus of settlement up near the sea bank and the fields and grazing lands running away to the south. These grazing lands were claimed from the freshwater fen early in the medieval period.

The photograph shows Walpole's drove road. We are looking north and the sea is on the horizon. The A47 runs at right angles to the drove just off the bottom of the picture, and Walpole Highway is a little south of that. Walpole St Peter is in the trees top left. The droves themselves, which had been wide green tracks, were subject to enclosure in the final years of the eighteenth century. Metalled roadways were set out, usually down the middle of the droves, leaving narrow enclosed plots of land on either side. Some of these plots survive, often now with houses built on them, but generally the tendency in recent years has been for these small strips to be merged into neighbouring fields which run right up to the road.

Halvergate Marshes

Landscapes
15

TG 450 095

'Halvergate Marshes' is the name generally given to the great expanse of drained marshland to the west of Great Yarmouth. This entire area was once an estuary, into which the main rivers of eastern Norfolk discharged. This gradually silted up in the post-Roman period, partly as a result of changing land/sea levels, and partly as a consequence of the build-up of a sand spit across its mouth, on which the town of Yarmouth (visible in the far distance) soon became established. Its last vestiges survive as Breydon Water (distance, right). Isolated farms appeared on the marsh from the ninth century and portions of land were progressively embanked, especially as sea levels rose in the course of the Middle Ages. Initially, sheep were grazed in vast numbers here, but from the fifteenth century cattle became more important. By the end of the seventeenth century the marsh was mainly used for fattening black cattle brought by drovers from Scotland or Ireland.

The complex network of drainage dykes shown here in part perpetuates the natural pattern of salt marsh drainage. But many new channels were added in the course of the medieval and post-medieval periods. From the late seventeenth century, drainage windmills were erected on the marsh, and by the early nineteenth century around thirty were in existence here. A number of examples, including Stracey Arms Mill, can be seen in the photograph. The straight, parallel features running across the centre of the photograph are the 'Acle Straight' - the Norwich to Yarmouth turnpike road, opened in 1834 - and the Norwich to Yarmouth railway line of 1883.

This magnificent landscape came under threat in the 1980s, when certain areas were converted to arable. Halvergate then became Britain's first 'Environmentally Sensitive Area' and the majority of the marsh remains under grass today.

Landscapes

16 Berney Arms Mill, Reedham, and Breydon Water

TG 465 049 Open

Berney Arms Mill was built in 1865 and, with a total height of 22m, is the tallest drainage mill in Broadland. Today it stands in isolation beside the river Yare, close to the southern end of Breydon Water, but originally it formed part of an extensive complex of industrial activity: the cement works established by Thomas Trench Berney in the early nineteenth century. This produced cement from chalk brought by wherry down river from quarries at Whitlingham near Norwich. By the late nineteenth century the works included cottages, kilns, and even a chapel. The mill was used to grind the cement after it had been baked in the kilns, but its other function was to drain the adjacent areas of marshland. (Vol.1: 112)

Like most drainage mills, the Berney Arms Mill drove a scoop wheel which lifted water from a low-level mill dyke, over the embankment or 'wall', and into the river beyond. This scoop wheel is a particularly large one, with a diameter of 7.3m, and (unusually) is located in a detached housing which can be seen slightly to the left of the mill in the picture. Now valued as a timeless part of Broadland's heritage, when first built the mill was an up-to-date piece of industrial plant, equipped with self-regulating patent sails and a fantail at the rear, which kept the cap pointed in the direction of the wind.

Drainage mills first appeared in Broadland in the seventeenth century and continued to be erected into the early twentieth. Some were still operating as late as the 1950s, but wind drainage was gradually rendered redundant by diesel engines and, in particular, by electrically-driven pumps - like that housed in the small brick building to the right of the mill.

Wretham Heath

Landscapes
17

TL 909 879 Open

This attractive view of the Wretham Heath Nature Reserve includes three of the Breckland meres: Ringmere in the foreground, Fenmere beyond, and Langmere in the background. The main road in the foreground is the A1075, two miles north-east of the junction with the A11. Breckland is a very distinctive part of Norfolk and its character is linked to its infertile sandy soils lying over chalk. Traditionally it has been a rabbit warren, then large-scale arable farming managed by the landlords from the local great houses in parks, whilst this century much has been planted with conifers by the Forestry Commission. The edges of such plantations can be seen in the top left corner, but the dominant woodland here is the natural deciduous woodland, kept open by grazing and fire with extensive areas of heath dominated by heather, rough grass and invasive bracken - a rich green in this view.

In places hollows have developed in the underlying chalk and these allow a thicker and wetter layer of sand which gradually dissolves away the chalk. This encourages further subsidence and stronger migration of water towards the hollow, so that over thousands of years hollows deep enough to intersect the water table within the chalk have developed. Their predominantly circular form confirms the role of solution and subsidence in their formation. In recent years periods of drought have often led to them drying up completely, only to refill as rain restores the ground water held within the chalk. Usually the water level in the meres tends to lag behind the wet winters which restore ground water supplies and they are often most full in early to mid-summer - this view dates from mid July, 1981, when the water table was unusually high.

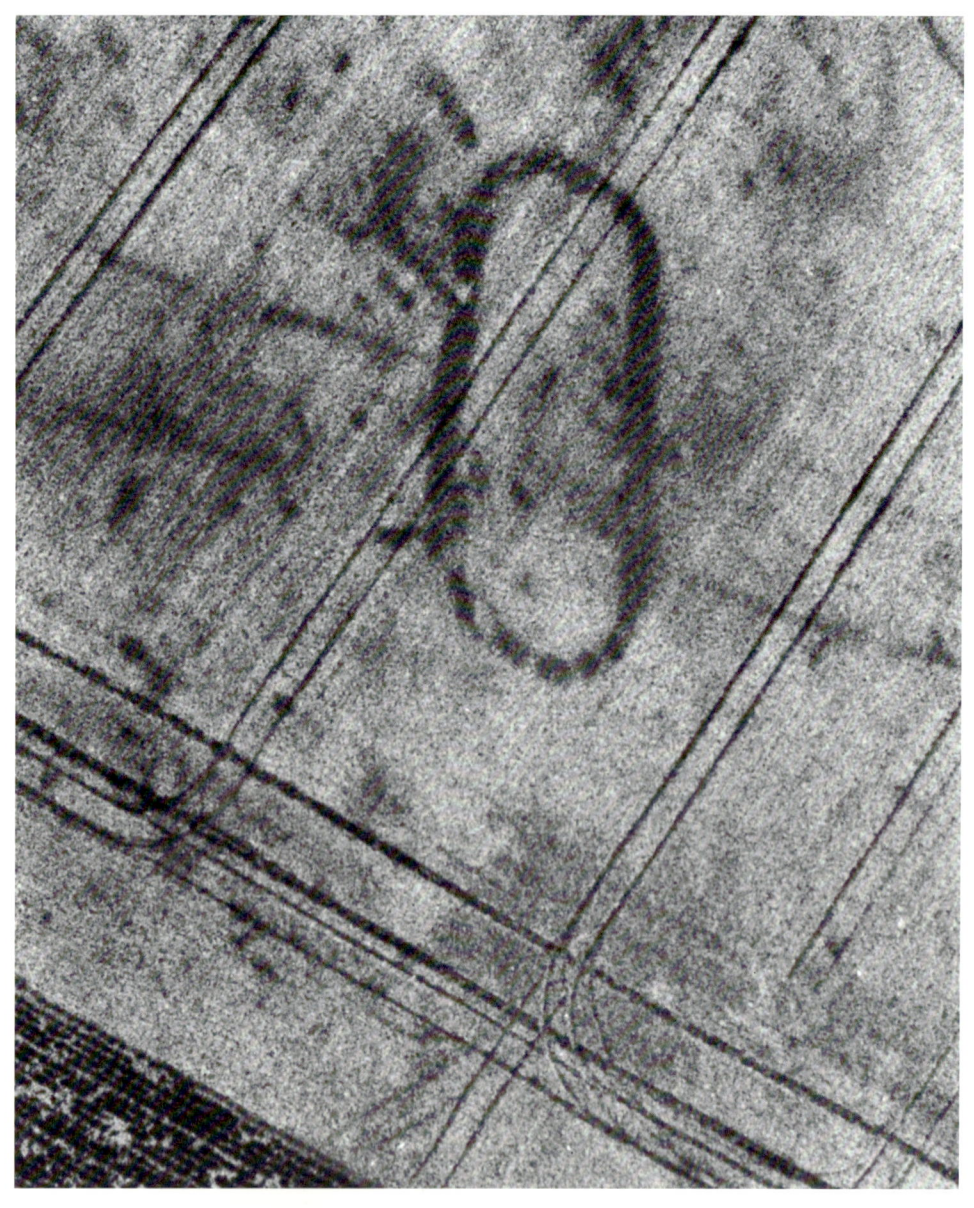

Neolithic and Bronze Age

18 Tuttington long barrow

TG 235 268

The adoption of the Neolithic farming way of life by people in Britain may well have been a gradual development during the fifth and fourth millennia BC rather than a sudden transformation. It would, however, have redefined the relationships which communities held with the land itself. Long barrows are burial monuments of this era. They may have been important in commemorating peoples' origins and ancestry, and in establishing their title to land, perhaps as 'store-houses' for generations of ancestors and as prominent territorial markers. Some excavated examples have produced little or no evidence of actual burials, and it is possible that human burial was only one of a range of ceremonial activities carried out at these sites.

This monument was completely unknown until 1996, a reminder of how centuries of agriculture have concealed the county's prehistoric past. It was c.30m long, and spoil from the surrounding ditch would have been used to raise the mound itself. The crop-mark of the ditch at the east end is interrupted in at least six places. It is common for the main entrances or ceremonial foci of long barrows to be at one end or the other, and these gaps might represent a series of entrances or causeways across the ditch to reach the central area. Alternatively this 'interrupted ditch' might actually be a series of large post-pits, forming part of a timber version of the stone entrance 'facades' which are found in many of the great long barrows of Wiltshire and the Severn Valley. A pair of crop-mark ditches crosses the monuments at right angles. Either they were interrupted by the earthwork or they were dug 'up and over' it, the crop-mark then being destroyed when the mound was ploughed away. While they may be no more than traces of later field boundaries, it is possible that they form part of a cursus, a later Neolithic/Bronze Age ceremonial monument defined by parallel ditches, as at Hanworth (20).

Coltishall possible causewayed enclosure

Neolithic and Bronze Age

TG 251 219

Causewayed enclosures were constructed by Neolithic communities during the fourth millennium BC. They were defined by ditches - either a single circuit or a series of two or more concentric features. Although at many sites the spoil from digging these ditches was used to build banks or ramparts, it is unlikely that their main importance was defensive. This is because the ditches were invariably broken by many interruptions or causeways, giving the site-type its name. Furthermore, although some famous examples occur on hilltops, many of them were not sited in naturally defensible locations. Prehistorians believe that they were meeting- or assembly-places, used at frequent or infrequent intervals for ceremonial and ritual acts and for trade and exchange. Excavations at many sites have found quantities of pottery, animal bone and other finds in the fills of the ditches, sometimes deposited with careful, 'ritual' precision. Human remains have sometimes been found too, and some sites clearly saw the disposal of corpses and veneration of the dead.

This site at Coltishall lies on a bluff overlooking the River Bure. It was discovered only recently by Derek Edwards, another example of how many Norfolk monuments remain undetected. Due to differing crop cover across the site, only the eastern half of the single enclosing ditch is visible; this is interrupted by at least three clearly-visible 'causeways'. Linear crop-marks crossing the site are probably the remains of later field boundaries. Behind the enclosure the narrow-gauge Bure Valley Railway runs from left to right.

The two Norfolk causewayed enclosures known to date, Coltishall and Roughton (Vol.1: 7), are both rather unusual in being circular - more amorphous shapes are much more common elsewhere in Britain - and in being defined by only *one* interrupted ditch rather than several. Neither site has ever been dated conclusively by excavation, and it is conceivable that they actually represent hengiform monuments of some kind dating to the third, rather than to the fourth millennium BC, like the henge at Arminghall (21).

Neolithic and Bronze Age

20 Hanworth cursus and round barrows

TG 206 359

Aerial photography has revealed many previously-unrecognized cursuses over the last seventy years. They were first recognised on the ground over two hundred years ago by the antiquarian William Stukeley during his fieldwork in the west of England. Stukeley called them cursus monuments, thinking they were ancient racetracks, and his term has been retained by today's prehistorians. Cursus monuments were defined by parallel banks and ditches. Some were elongated rectangular enclosures of relatively modest scale, others extended over several kilometres. Some of them were set out along astronomically-significant alignments, especially relating to solstice or equinox. There were many variations between these monuments; some were laid out and constructed in one co-ordinated operation, while others were built or extended piecemeal and show few signs of subsequent 'maintenance'.

The best Norfolk example yet recorded is this splendid feature, discovered in 1992. The parallel ditches, some 50m apart, have been laid out with care. The south end of the cursus, marked by a transverse ditch and 'playing-card' corners, features a broad entrance causeway. The total length of the cursus is not known. At least three 'ring-ditches' are clearly visible, representing large plough-flattened Neolithic or Bronze Age round barrows. All of these show traces of smaller inner ring-ditches. Many cursus monuments clearly had funerary associations; human remains have sometimes been found, while groups of barrows sometimes follow the line of the cursus itself. These barrows may have been erected before or after the cursus, and the two monument types were not necessarily in use simultaneously.

Arminghall henge, Bixley

Neolithic and Bronze Age

TG 239 060

Along with the cursus another 'new' type of field monument, the henge, appeared in the later Neolithic period around 3000 BC. These are circular earthwork enclosures, usually with one or more entrances. Like causewayed enclosures (19), they are seldom defensible - indeed the spoil from digging the encircling ditch was often used to erect a bank immediately *outside*, rather than inside, the ditch. Excavation within the enclosure rarely uncovers signs of occupation, and they were probably used as religious or ceremonial centres. Stonehenge is the most famous of many whose plans were clearly dictated by solar and lunar events. In eastern England they are often sited at river confluences, sometimes in groups, and this, too, may have been of religious significance. The Arminghall henge (Vol.1: 8) is no exception to this, lying at the meeting-place of Norfolk's three main east-flowing rivers. It may also have been accompanied by at least one other henge, represented by the large double ring-ditch situated only 800m to the south west at Caistor (22).

The site at Bixley was first identified when photographed from the air by Wing Commander Insall in 1929, and excavations by Professor J. D. G. Clark followed promptly. The outer ditch is c.80m in diameter, and slight traces of an external bank can still be seen. As well as studying the concentric ditches, Clark excavated the whole of the central area and examined the horseshoe of eight enormous 'postholes' which enclosed it. These were up to 3m deep and once held the bases of timber uprights fashioned from whole mature oak trees. It is not known if these were unadorned or if they were carved and painted. The heart of the monument produced very few finds; it is unlikely to have been a dwelling site, and many henge monuments may have been used, even for ritual purposes, only occasionally or intermittently. The Arminghall henge remained significant long after its construction, however, and many round barrows were built around it on the surrounding low hills over the following millennium.

Neolithic and Bronze Age

22 Caistor St Edmund Bronze Age double ring-ditch and D-shaped enclosure TG 232 053

The manner in which many late Neolithic/Bronze Age henge monuments occur in clusters at river confluences has already been discussed with reference to the Arminghall henge (21). This magnificent double ring-ditch at Caistor lies only *c*.800m to the south west of the Arminghall monument, above floor-level in the narrow tongue of land separating the Yare and the Tas at the point where they converge, and may well be another example of a site chosen for its possible religious significance. While it is smaller than the Arminghall henge, being only *c*.60m in diameter, the strength of the crop-mark suggests that the ditches were major features. If the round crop-mark is indeed that of a henge monument then the smaller inner ring-ditch may well have defined an inner area comparable to that within the horseshoe of eight huge 'posts' at the Arminghall Henge. The great D-shaped enclosure, lying immediately to its south west and pointing away from the river confluence to the north, is unparalleled in Norfolk. It lies almost in contact with the ring-ditch's south-western side, and the two monuments surely form part of one complex. The function of the D-shaped feature is unknown, but the absence of visible crop-marks of pits or post-holes within it suggests that it did not enclose a settlement. The site remains under cultivation, and has seen neither excavation nor surface survey work.

Harpley round barrows

Neolithic and Bronze Age

23

TF 766 279

Round barrows - burial monuments dating to the later Neolithic period and the Bronze Age (*c.*3000-1500 BC) - are the most numerous of Norfolk's known prehistoric sites. They are important as the earliest known monuments which preserve the remains of individuals or groups of individuals. As such they are unlike the earlier long barrows where the remains of the dead are often intermixed, the 'ancestors' perhaps being venerated *en masse* rather than as individual people (18 and **Vol.1: 6, 7**). Most of Norfolk's few remaining upstanding barrows have escaped plough destruction due to their situation in woods or on the county's diminishing tracts of heathland. Those at Harpley are unusual in lying preserved in arable land. As Scheduled Ancient Monuments, they are legally protected from ploughing; each is surrounded by eight large concrete markers to guard against encroaching cultivation.

Barrows often had complex histories, sometimes with episodes of burial over a period of several hundred years. Both inhumation and cremation were practised, sometimes in the same barrow. Barrow burial was only accorded to a minority. Although barrows are more abundant than other prehistoric monument-types, calculations and projections have shown that there are not enough of them to account for the entire Norfolk population over a period of a thousand years or more - especially since other finds show that the county's Early Bronze Age population was large and dynamic! Men, women and children of all ages were interred within them, suggesting the burial of family groups. During the third millennium BC there are signs that prehistoric societies in Britain were more complex and hierarchical than before. Barrows may have been built to mark the burial places of 'aristocratic' or other powerful people and their relatives. It is possible, however, that these people were important to society in some manner which is less obvious to modern eyes; for example, they may have been members of a group or caste which had some spiritual or religious significance.

Neolithic and Bronze Age

24, 25 Caistor St Edmund crop-marks before and after excavation
TG 224 042

Numerous 'ring-ditches' recorded by aerial photography over the last seventy years show that many round barrows were constructed on the hills around the confluence of the rivers Yare and Tas during the third millennium BC. They indicate that a major barrow cemetery grew up around the Arminghall henge (21), which lay in the valley bottom at the confluence itself. The series of seven ring-ditches at Harford Farm, located on high ground c.1km to the north-east of Roman *Venta Icenorum*, was first recorded by H. Frederick Low in 1933 and has been photographed several time subsequently (only four of them may be seen clearly in the 1974 crop-mark photograph reproduced here). During the early 1970s it became clear that this site was threatened by the construction of a future Norwich southern bypass. Fifteen years of planning and preparation culminated in the building of the road during 1990-92, and this was preceded by excavations by the Norfolk Archaeological Unit during 1989-91.

The great size of the two largest ring-ditches - both of them over 40m in diameter - led to suggestions that they represented prehistoric settlement ringworks rather than burial mounds, but excavation showed that they were indeed flattened barrows. Radiocarbon age-ranges from inhumation burials extend through the period 3000 to 2000 BC. The large ring-ditch on the right-hand side of the photograph is of the type known as a 'disc barrow', featuring a small central mound defined by the inner ring-ditch. A burial from this monument was laid to rest on a bier resembling a shallow-draughted boat; another was accompanied by glass-paste heads, suggesting that this unusual barrow was somewhat later than its neighbours and dated to the period around 1500 BC.

The hilltop site was occupied by an Iron Age settlement during the first millennium BC - it appears that Iron Age post-hole buildings stood in the spaces between the still-standing Bronze Age barrow mounds - but subsequently it seems to have been used for burial again. A series of small square enclosures cross the site in a north-to-south line; it is suggested that these were the remains of small square 'barrows' dating to the late Iron Age period, although no graves survived for study. During the Anglo-Saxon period two of the prehistoric barrows became foci for cemeteries, which were probably in use around AD700. On the vertical air view of the site under excavation seven of these graves may clearly be seen in the area immediately to the south of the top/northernmost ring-ditch. Most of the forty-six Anglo-Saxon graves recorded were sparsely furnished. However, a small proportion contained remarkable jewellery items of gold and silver, including rings, pendants and a disc brooch with inlaid garnets and glass. Both the date of the cemetery and the type of burial rite employed suggest that the people buried here were Christians. Their identity is unclear, but it is possible that they were connected with a Middle Saxon revival of the old Roman town of *Venta Icenorum* nearby.

Neolithic and Bronze Age

Caistor St Edmund crop-marks before and after excavation   TG 224 042

Iron Age

26 Narborough Iron Age fort

TF 750 130

At Narborough are the remains of a large earthwork enclosure which is one of a group of Iron Age forts in west Norfolk. The others are at Warham St Mary (**Vol.1: 12**), South Creake (**Vol.1: 13**), Holkham (**Vol.1: 14**) and Thetford (**Vol.1: 15**). There is also another possible one at Tasburgh in the east (**27**).

Narborough is strategically situated on a low plateau, close to the crossing of the River Nar by the Icknield Way. The single bank and ditch form an irregular oval shape, enclosing 1.56ha. Much of the west side of the site (to the right of the picture) has now been levelled. This was the result of enlargement to an adjacent lake in the early years of the nineteenth century. Trees and vegetation now cover the whole site.

The original entrance was in the south-east, measuring 10m to 15m wide, where the earthworks open onto a causeway. The bank and ditches are best preserved on the north and north-east sides, where the height from the top of the bank to the bottom of the ditch is now between 3.90m and 4.90m. The fort has not been excavated. Among the few finds to have been recovered are Iron Age pottery sherds, worked flints and burnt flint. As a result, it is not yet possible to date the construction closely within the Iron Age period.

The strategic location of the fort, overlooking the Fens to the west, would have been an important reason for its construction. All the forts of west Norfolk are similarly situated at boundary positions and they may also have performed some ritual purpose at these important locations.

Tasburgh fort

Iron Age

27

TM 199 960 Open

Tasburgh hill fort is a successful conservation project which deserves to be more widely known. This site near Tasburgh church was purchased by the Norfolk Archaeological Trust in 1994 when it was put down to grass to prevent further plough damage and then opened to public access. The field is now grazed by sheep, and there is wheel chair access through specially designed kissing gates.

The site has been tentatively interpreted as an Iron Age hill fort, like those at Warham (Vol.1: 12) and Narborough (26), but in the absence of any occupation evidence proven to be contemporary with the earthworks which surround the field, the monument remains an enigma. Excavations between 1975 and 1980 undertaken during an extension to the churchyard produced occupation evidence from the eighth century onwards, and it has been suggested that the earthworks may be Danish or belong to the re-conquest of the Danelaw in the early tenth century. Careful searching for surface finds has not produced any artefacts to help unravel the puzzle. Until there has been further excavation of the defences the debate will continue.

There is an impressive northern bank buried in the left-hand hedgerow and the outline of the bank continues along the front of the picture as a wide strip of light soil. The line of the defences then continues to the right and follows the right-hand churchyard boundary, thus enclosing the church within the defences.

The church is also well worth a visit. It has a fine eleventh-century tower and internal archway into the nave.

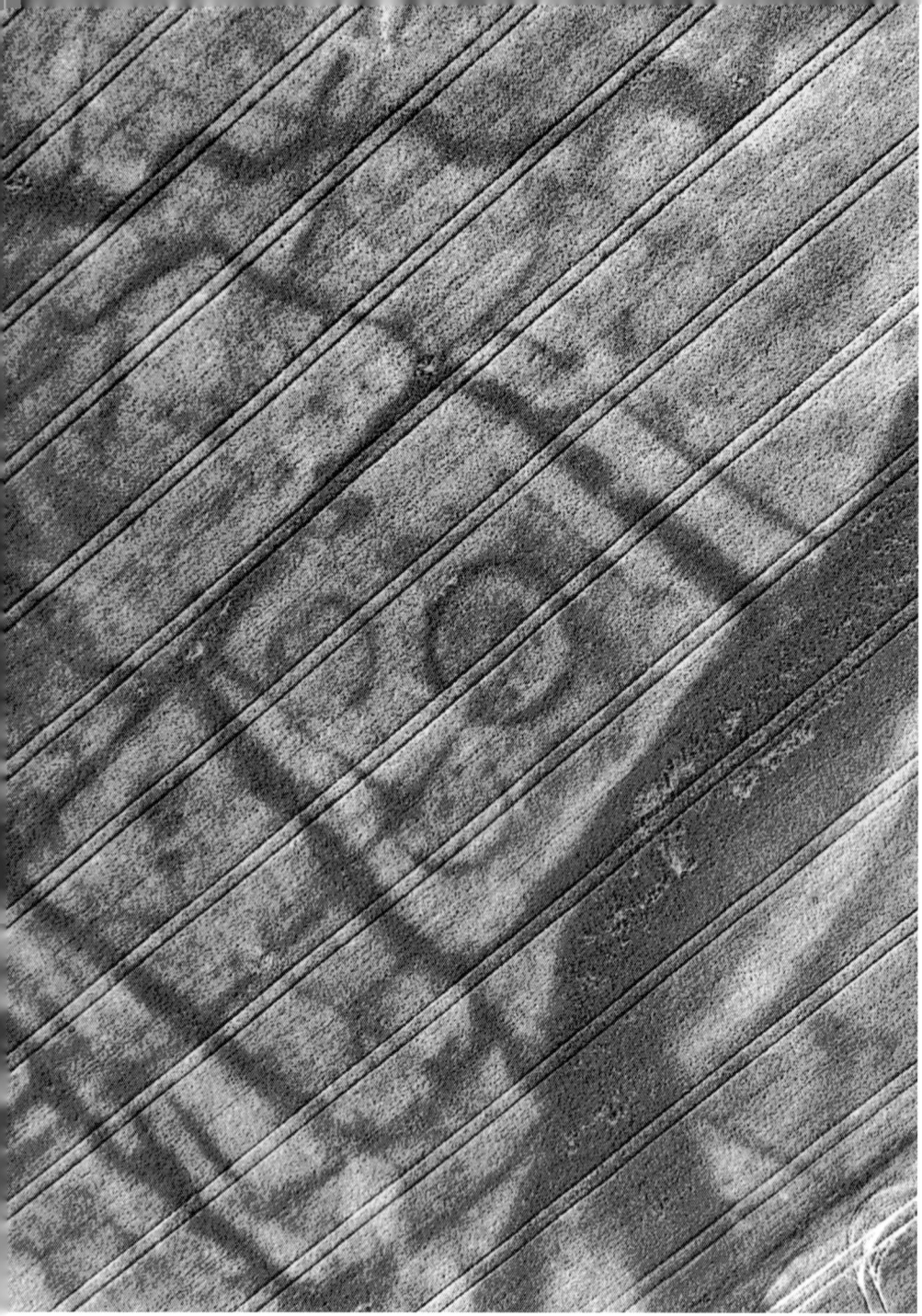

Iron Age

28 Heacham enclosure and hut circles

TF 669 385

Although Iron Age and Roman Norfolk was densely populated with large numbers of small rural farmsteads, crop-mark evidence for these is relatively slight compared to that of ploughsoil scatters of pottery, coins and metalwork. Thus, the Heacham enclosure represents a settlement type which must have been very common, but which is rarely seen from the air, at least in Norfolk.

At the heart of this small farming settlement is a square ditched enclosure containing three circles. These are not themselves round-houses, but the eaves-drip and drainage gullies which surrounded round-houses built of timber and with thatched roofs. Inside the circles there are hints of pits or large post-holes, which may well be structural.

Although these buildings are very typical of 'native' settlements, in the Iron Age rather than the Roman tradition, it would be quite incorrect to think of them as primitive huts. Indeed, these were probably quite complex buildings, comfortable to live in, highly decorated or ornamented, and with separate areas for sleeping, cooking, crafts and recreation. If all three buildings were for domestic occupation, then an extended family could have been accommodated. Alternatively, some of the buildings may have been for storage.

The enclosure, which probably dates to the Late Iron Age or the early Roman period, is surrounded by crop-marks of field systems, enclosures and droveways. Apart from the archaeological features visible on this remarkable record of the landscape around two thousand years ago, a broad dark channel and thinner sinuous crop-marks represent former watercourses which may well have been active at the time, while the parallel lines in the crop from a tractor provide an indication of scale.

Bintree late Iron Age/early Roman enclosure
TF 999 232 — Roman 29

This is one of a group of nine distinctive enclosures which are known across the northern half of the county, but which have not been seen elsewhere in Icenian tribal territory. Despite the fact that three sites, at Thornham, Warham and Wighton have been partially excavated, their precise date and function(s) are still a matter for speculation. Possibilities include settlements for the native aristocracy or religious enclosures.

All nine sites have features in common, suggesting that they share a common purpose and chronology. Square or rectangular in shape, with rounded corners, a single substantial ditch encloses an area of around 0.25ha. Despite a passing resemblance to a Roman fort with its 'playing card' corners (32/33 and 34), there is nothing Roman or military about these sites, and they are clearly the product of native planning and workmanship, although possibly inspired by Roman military architecture.

Within the landscape, they are carefully sited, without exception occupying relatively elevated ground (for Norfolk), with commanding views over river valleys or the sea. Where entrances are known from excavation or visible as crop-marks - the Bintree enclosure has two, on adjacent sides - these face away from the valleys and open out onto relatively flat plateaux. This rules out a purely defensive or offensive function, which would certainly have taken advantage of the naturally defensive barrier of the contours by positioning any entrances to face down slope.

Only the site at Thornham is securely dated, to the period shortly after the Roman conquest in AD43. The most likely historical context is therefore the period between the conquest and the Boudican rebellion (AD60), a time during which the Iceni enjoyed the status of a Client Kingdom, allies of Rome and allowed to run their own affairs. Perhaps one development during this time resulted in the construction of these sites by the leaders of one part of the tribe.

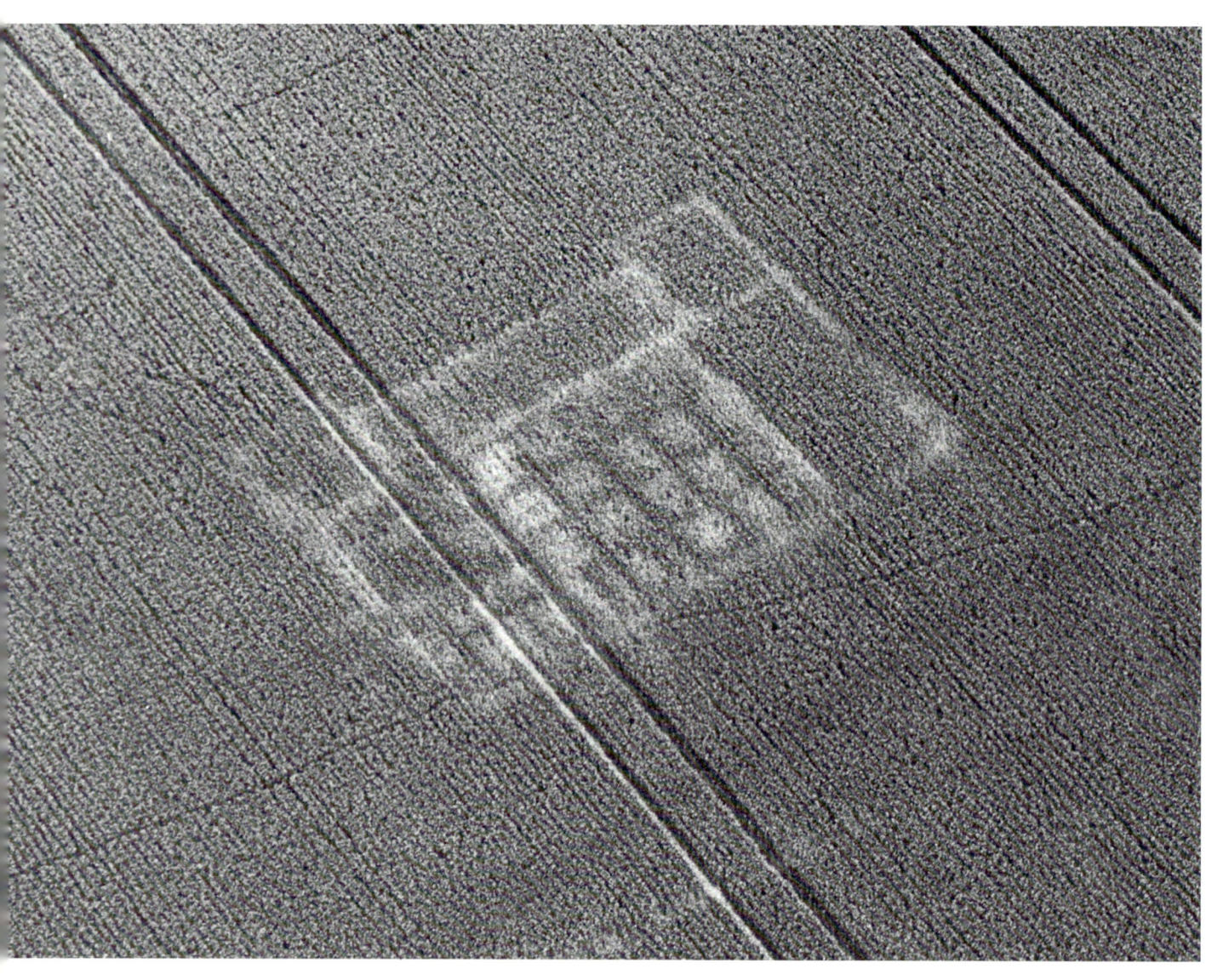

Roman villa near Swaffham

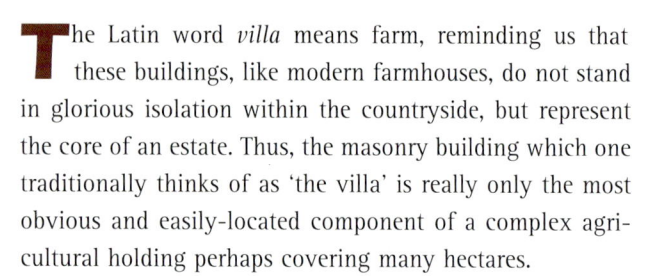

The Latin word *villa* means farm, reminding us that these buildings, like modern farmhouses, do not stand in glorious isolation within the countryside, but represent the core of an estate. Thus, the masonry building which one traditionally thinks of as 'the villa' is really only the most obvious and easily-located component of a complex agricultural holding perhaps covering many hectares.

Most villas were built and lived in by members of the local aristocracy, wealthy local landowners and their families. These were people who had prospered under Roman rule by farming or some other lucrative activity, and expressed their new-found wealth in a Roman-style masonry building, with central heating, baths, wall paintings and mosaic floors.

This particular building stands within a large walled enclosure, part of which shows as a faint mark running at an angle across the bottom right-hand corner of the photograph. The most obvious feature of the building itself is the central hypocaust for an under-floor heating system, with the floors supported upon large square masonry blocks. The fact that these show so clearly suggests that the floors, possibly mosaics, have been ploughed up or collapsed into the voids beneath.

The central area was probably living rooms, with the side rooms and projecting 'wings' including bedrooms, studies, the kitchen and servants' quarters. A corridor running along the front of the building allowed independent access into the various rooms. It is quite conceivable that the main parts of the building were two-storied.

If not included in the main building, the establishment may also have incorporated a separate bath-house. These were often detached, as a sensible precaution against fire. The large courtyard might also have included a number of agricultural buildings, such as stores, stables, barns, cart-sheds and cattle-stalls, all probably of timber.

Hockwold-cum-Wilton Roman settlement

Roman

31

TF 754 872

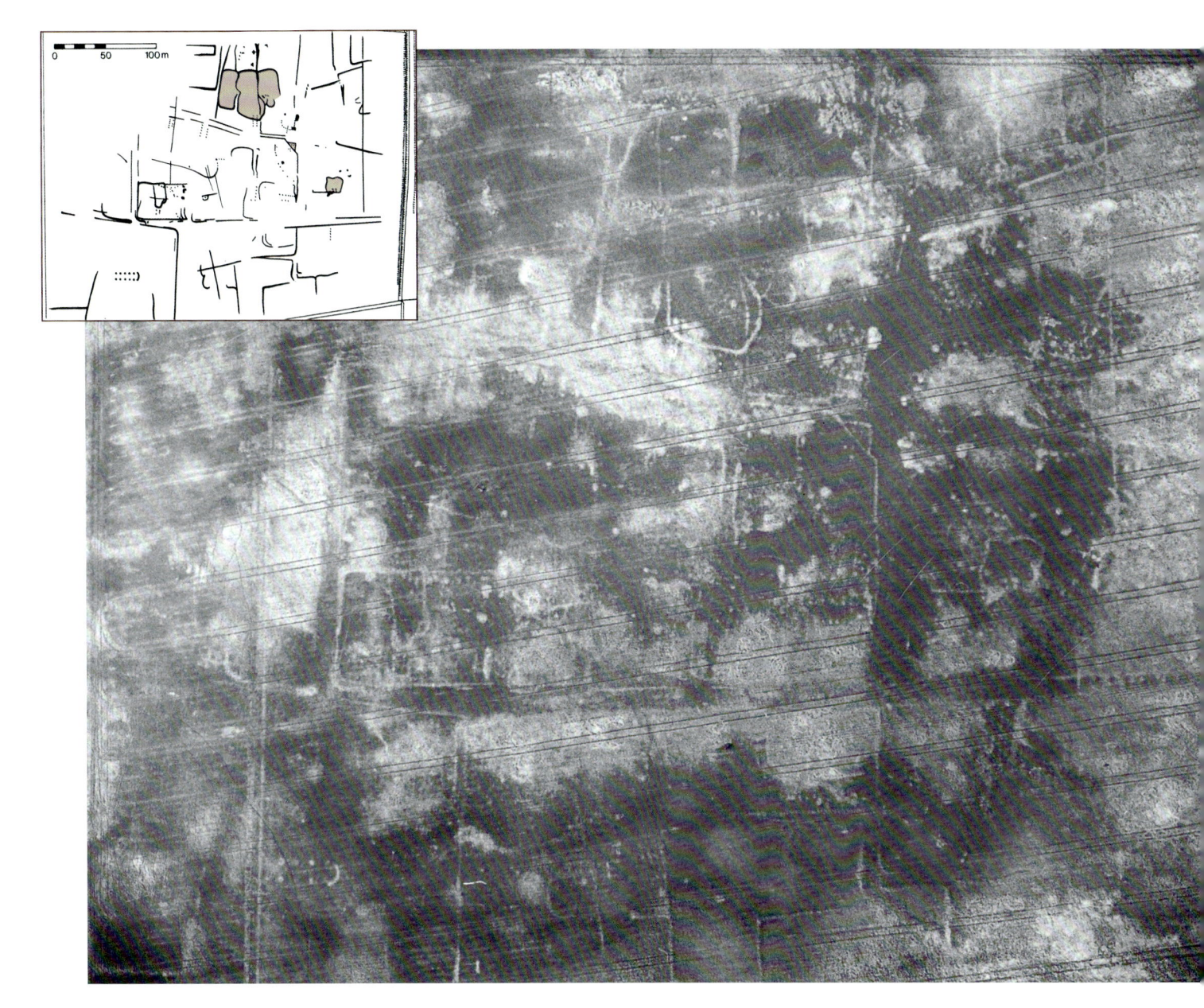

The fen-edge in south-west Norfolk has produced evidence for prehistoric and Romano-British rural settlement, the intensity of which is unparalleled elsewhere in the county. The principal reason for this is topographical, with the narrow band of sand-hills between the ancient edge of the fen and the upland providing a most attractive area for occupation. Here, contrasting geological and environmental zones were exploited, with easy access to the upland for cereal cultivation, and the lush meadows of the fens for livestock, as well as fish, eels, wildfowl, reed, peat and salt.

The principal crop-marks consist of a network of roads and tracks, generally running east-to-west along sandy or gravelly ridges and set against a background of light sandy patches and darker pockets of peat. At one 'crossroads', an enigmatic triangular enclosure may have been set aside for an important statue or monument.

Other ditches mark out what are probably property boundaries, while to the top of the photograph three conjoined enclosures are probably paddocks or folds for livestock. Lines of post-pits indicate the sites of at least six rectangular timber buildings, and although the evidence from small-scale excavations increases the number of buildings known on the site to fourteen, there must be many more as yet undiscovered.

In 1957 a hoard of priestly headgear was ploughed up near to a small squareish crop-mark towards the right of the photograph. Excavation revealed a timber building which, if not itself a temple, certainly had religious connections. The finds suggest that Mars as a warrior or fertility god was worshipped here, together with the exotic eastern cult of Attis and Cybele. Here, in the fourth century, while Christianity was becoming established as the principal and official religion of the Roman Empire, pagan activity was flourishing.

32, 33 Saham Toney Roman fort

Roman

TF 887 006

During the first century AD, Saham Toney was one of the sites at the forefront of Roman military activity in the region, with not just one but two forts. From the military point of view, this was a critical strategic location, at a river crossing and also controlling the intersection of two major Roman roads.

A Romano-British settlement at Saham Toney has been known since the mid-nineteenth century but it has never been explored by excavation. What is known of the site comes from a combination of chance finds and observations, systematic fieldwalking and metal-detecting over more than two decades and, most recently, from cropmarks.

There is circumstancial evidence in the form of Icenian coins and brooches of some sort of Iron Age settlement around the river crossing in the period AD 0 to 50. This may have developed into a *vicus* or civilian settlement around the forts. Later, when the military had gone, the site acted as a market or small town until the end of the Roman period (*c.*AD400).

The earliest fort, almost certainly of the 40s AD, has never been visible on aerial photographs. Its position is known from many finds of early Roman coins and military metalwork on high ground south of the Blackwater or Watton Brook. It may date to the invasion of AD43 or to the period of a minor uprising by the Iceni against Roman rule four years later.

The presence of the second fort, illustrated here in colour and black and white, was not suspected until 1987 when just one rounded corner provided a clue as to what might

Saham Toney Roman fort	Roman
TF 887 006	**33** N

be there. Then, after many years of reconnaissance, the extent of the fort was finally revealed in 1996, but only for two days before the cropmarks disappeared, perhaps never to be seen again. Although it is as yet undated, it most probably belongs to the 60s AD, built in response to the Boudican rebellion. Curiously, it does not re-use the site of the earlier fort, so perhaps all traces of this had already vanished. Instead, it occupied a larger site (c.5.6ha) north of the stream and around Woodcock Hall.

When this fort was established, the Peddars Way Roman road (Vol.1: 24) was diverted slightly and the new path of the road is clearly visible as a light band running into the fort from the left. This passes through an entrance across three ditches which are visible in four different fields and crops, even as a dark band running through potatoes to the right. The two inner ditches were probably palisade trenches for a timber rampart, with one large open ditch beyond. The fort has the normal rounded 'playing card' corners except for one where, unusually, the corner has been cut off diagonally where it runs near the stream. On the south side of the fort, where the Peddars Way enters it, an external square enclosure, defined by a single ditch, was possibly an annexe for horses.

Roman

34 Swanton Morley Roman fort

TG 012 192

During the rebellion by Boudica in AD60 and in its aftermath, the Roman military presence in Norfolk was unprecedented in scale and unparalleled in its ruthless suppression of any hints of further native resistance. During this period, large numbers of military units would have been stationed at strategic locations throughout the Icenian territory, controlling road and river crossings, in this instance the nearby River Wensum.

Early Roman forts are known at Cawston (Vol.1: 19), Saham Toney (32, 33) and here at Swanton Morley. There are marching camps at Horstead with Stanninghall (Vol.1: 18), Barton Bendish and Spixworth. While it is possible that some of these date to the conquest period of the mid 40s AD, the generally pro-Roman attitude of the Iceni before AD60 meant that no significant military presence in Norfolk was necessary. Thus, the majority of forts and marching camps may date to c.AD60.

Although some of the Swanton Morley fort has been destroyed by old gravel pits, on one side the triple ditches (or ditch and palisade trenches for a timber rampart) and an entrance are clearly visible, as are the rounded corners of the opposite side. A modern hedge line neatly divides the fort diagonally into two.

The site has produced a remarkable collection of surface finds, recorded systematically over several decades. The coins are mainly contemporary copies of official bronze coins of the emperor Claudius used to pay the army, and which were produced with official sanction at a time when the supply of regular coins was inadequate. In addition to a wide range of military metalwork, quantities of civilian (Icenian) objects suggest that the Roman military were engaged in the recycling of native metalwork, probably collected from a battlefield.

Caistor St Edmund Roman town

Roman 35

TG 230 035 Open

During the Roman period the major town in northern East Anglia was situated at Caistor St Edmund, 5km to the south of Norwich. It was the tribal capital of the Iceni, performing an administrative role and representing Roman authority across the region. Its Roman name, *Venta Icenorum*, means 'market place of the Iceni'.

Venta was founded next to the River Tas during the 60s AD and was occupied until the end of Roman Britain. There were obviously many developments during that period of 350 years, the most visible of which was the construction of massive defensive walls during the final 140 years or so of Roman occupation. The rectangular walled circuit survives today and shows clearly from the air, dotted with trees along much of its length.

The area of the late Roman walled town covers 14ha, but when the initial street grid was laid out it was intended that the town should be much larger. The early Roman street grid pattern can be seen to extend beyond the area confined by the late walls (**Vol.1: 22**). The rectangular plan was bisected by two main streets which joined the four gateways. The town was then divided into a series of smaller blocks called *insulae*, which were separated by side streets. Another street, which runs diagonally from the town centre towards the north east, does not align with the others and may have been constructed earlier than the main street grid.

The River Tas, which now meanders adjacent to the western boundary of the town, was originally wide and deep enough to provide access to medium-sized boats which allowed goods to be traded with coastal ports and beyond. The church of St Edmund, dating from the eleventh century, is situated within the south-east angle of the walls and may supersede an earlier church founded in Roman times.

Roman

36 Caistor St Edmund early defences

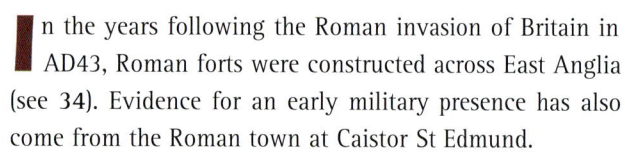

TG 232 031

In the years following the Roman invasion of Britain in AD43, Roman forts were constructed across East Anglia (see 34). Evidence for an early military presence has also come from the Roman town at Caistor St Edmund.

Aerial photography has revealed three possible military ditches running parallel to, and outside, the line of the later town walls on the south and east sides. Excavation to the south of the town by the Norfolk Archaeological Unit in 1997 was unable to date these features closely. The inner ditch was found to be V-shaped, with a depth of 2m. The middle ditch was shallower, at 1.3m, while the profile of the outer ditch was indistinct. These defences might have originally run down to the River Tas, on the west and north sides, forming a roughly square defensive enclosure.

Artefacts recovered from the centre of the walled town confirm an early military presence there. These include such items as harness and tunic fittings, as well as coins of Claudius known to have been carried by soldiers in the army of occupation during the mid first century. It seems probable that the ditches were originally constructed as part of a military fortress of the pre-, or immediately post-, Boudican period (AD60-61). Triple ditches were a feature of early military forts in this part of Britain and similar ditches have been recorded around the forts of Pakenham and Coddenham in Suffolk.

This photograph also shows the location of an Anglo-Saxon cemetery, just 350m to the east of the Roman town walls, which was used from the end of the Roman period and throughout the fifth century. Three hundred and seventy-six cremations and sixty inhumation burials were discovered during excavations there between 1932 and 1937.

Caistor St Edmund temple site and 'temenos'

Roman 37

TG 239 039

To the north east of the Roman town of *Venta Icenorum* at Caistor St Edmund a major pagan temple complex is known from crop-marks, surface finds and excavation.

A site of around 2.5ha was enclosed by a wall 0.75m wide and several metres tall, defining a sacred enclosure or *temenos*, two sides of which are visible as crop-marks. This was entered through a large monumental stone gateway or arch (now under the housing estate just visible at the top of the photograph) leading into the site from the west. The enclosure and the buildings inside it would have been clearly visible to anyone approaching from the north, and a temple site on this scale must have been the focus for an important cult or cults, though we have no clues at all as to what these might have been.

Inside the enclosure there were at least two stone buildings, both of which are clearly visible as crop-marks. Firstly, a Romano-Celtic temple of the usual concentric square plan like that at Wicklewood (38) had an outer corridor or ambulatory with a floor of flint cobbles. The inner *cella* was floored with small mosaic cubes made from grey limestone and the hard white chalk which occurs locally. It has been calculated that if the whole of the *cella* was floored with these, at least 317,000 cubes would have been required! Two dark patches in the interior mark the bases of altars. The second building consists of a villa-like structure, with a suite of rooms and a corridor running along one side. This was probably an ancillary building, perhaps a priest's or custodian's house, or a guest house for visitors to the shrine.

This was probably not a quiet place of worship like a modern church, but a site thronging with visitors, participating in rowdy religious festivals, fairs and other communal activities.

Roman

38 Wicklewood Romano-Celtic temple

TG 088 028

The Roman attitude to pagan religious cults was generally one of tolerance, and only practices which threatened public order or offended decency (such as human sacrifice) were unacceptable. This led to a fusion of Celtic gods and customs into Roman traditions, an assimilation which is referred to as 'Romano-Celtic' religion. Thus, a Celtic god like Toutatis could be linked with the nearest Roman counterpart, in this case Mars, and eventually the two might become indistinguishable and be worshipped as a single deity, Mars Toutatis.

A Romano-Celtic temple is one of the most easily-identified Roman buildings when seen from the air, as it has a very distinctive concentric square plan. This comprises a central shrine or *cella*, surrounded by an ambulatory. There are three possible above-ground reconstructions of this plan, the first of which consists of a tall central tower, with the ambulatory roof pitched against it at a lower level. The second possibility is that both *cella* and ambulatory had one all-over roof, while the third option is a *cella* open to the sky with a roofed ambulatory around it.

Four of these buildings are known in Norfolk. There are three at Caistor St Edmund, two inside the Roman town (Vol.1: 22) and one in the suburbs (37). The fourth example, pictured here as a crop-mark at Wicklewood, is associated with a nearby large Roman rural settlement or small town.

The temple was first noticed as a crop-mark in 1959, and it was partly excavated in the same year. The building's overall dimensions are approximately 15m by 17m. The internal walls of the *cella* were decorated with painted wall plaster, and the floor was probably of *tesserae* (large mosaic cubes made from tile). A large mortared foundation in the centre of the *cella* may have been a base for an altar or statue.

Wormegay stands on a former island on the eastern edge of the fenland south of King's Lynn. The island has the River Nar to the north and had peat-covered fen on the other sides.

In the photograph the outlines of the motte and bailey castle appear quite clearly, together with the modern village. The motte was the mound for the castle keep and the bailey was the defended enclosure attached to the keep. There is a similar fine motte and bailey at Horsford (Vol.1: 29). It appears that the castle here has intruded upon the original road pattern, as the village street is diverted around the bailey. The old alignment is continued as a ridge in pasture visible nearest the camera.

The castle commanded the western approaches to the island; the stream which separated it from the west is visible next to the castle together with the remains of a modern drainage ditch.

The Norman baron Hermer de Ferrieres held Wormegay in 1086 and he or his descendants, the Warennes and Bardolfs, built the castle. Archaeological evidence suggests that the village moved to the castle from an original site near the now isolated church away to the east. The Bardolfs held Wormegay as the chief place of their barony which was clustered mainly in West Norfolk with outliers elsewhere in the county and in north Suffolk. By the time the manor, through lack of heirs, came to the Crown in 1537 the castle had long been disused, and in 1544 'le halle yarde' (probably not the castle) and other items including the Park beyond the photograph were granted to a new owner, John Dethick.

Medieval castles

Wormegay Castle

TF 659 117

Medieval castles

40 Denton Castle

TM 264 894 Open

Denton Castle, seen here covered in trees, is quite small; the motte measures only 46m in diameter and the bailey some 60m from north to south. Now owned by the National Trust, it is remarkably well-preserved. There is an entrance to the bailey at its far end. The bailey is surrounded with a bank and ditch while the motte has a raised rim with a central depression. Without excavation one cannot be sure, but it is possible that this depression contained a timber keep.

The history of the castle is obscure; it was discovered only in 1850, shortly before the woodland in the rest of the field was felled. The castle is in a rather unusual location; although it stands on high ground on the edge of the parish, it does not command any important river crossing and may have been intended simply to safeguard property. It is likely to have been built by the d'Albinis when they came to Norfolk in the time of William II, between 1087 and 1100, before they moved to Old Buckenham and built the castle there.

The castle is close to Darrow Green; until 1850 it stood in Darrow or Dearhaugh Wood. Dearhaugh probably means 'enclosure where deer are found', and the term can be traced back to 1630.

Middleton Mount

Medieval castles

41

TF 660 164 Open

The Rev. Francis Blomefield, in his eighteenth-century *History of Norfolk*, recorded this as a 'high mount, grown over with bushes, which seems to have been some place of strength and moment in ancient days'. The feature, whose dimension can be judged by comparison with the height of surrounding buildings, is all that remains of a former castle: excavation has shown that it once possessed a small bailey in the foreground. When the surrounding housing estate was built, it was a condition of planning consent that the site of the bailey was left as open space. The castle had marshy ground on all sides except the foreground and was probably built to guard against approaches from the opposite direction. It was probably constructed at some time after the Conquest, although the period of unrest under Stephen (1135-54) is also a possibility, 'for every great man built him castles and held them against the King; and they filled the whole land with these castles', as the Anglo-Saxon Chronicler says.

The man who built this castle was probably one of the de Ecouis family whose manor was known in the fourteenth century as Castle Hall. In the fifteenth century a lord of the de Scales family built the large moated house at Tower End (**67**) away from the village, and by this time the castle must have been abandoned. Early eighteenth-century references mention 'Mountshill' but, by this time, its significance seems to have been largely forgotten.

Medieval castles

42 Mileham Castle

TF 916 193

In 1086 Mileham was a place of unusual significance. The King's holding here consisted of ten carucates of land (about 1200 acres or 486ha) and had a recorded population of 107. With outlying estates in Litcham and Dunham, the influence of Mileham extended to twenty other places in Norfolk, including a tiny part of Thetford.

The castle, at the centre of the photograph, includes a motte on which there is a small rectangular keep, covered here in trees. An inner bailey and the motte are surrounded by a circular outer earthwork clearly visible in the picture. The road runs very close to the outer earthwork and to the left of this are the remains of a large rectangular moat containing the site of the medieval Burghwood Manor and the modern Burwood Hall.

Count Alan of Brittany was son-in-law to William the Conqueror, and Mileham was passed to him. It seems likely it was Count Alan who built the castle, and it was last mentioned in 1154 when, with the manor, it was obtained by King Stephen in exchange for much property.

Archaeological fieldwork in the village has shown that the original focus of settlement in the Anglo-Saxon period was at the eastern end of the village, around the church which lies in the distance just beyond the greenhouses. As the population grew, so the village expanded westwards down towards the castle. Today the village is centred further west, at the bottom of the picture, and the medieval areas are largely unoccupied.

Castle Acre - castle, town and church

Medieval castles

43

TF 818 151 Open

The castle, town and priory lie on the south facing slope of the valley of the west-flowing River Nar. The castle earthworks were cut deep into the chalk which provided both chalk rock (clunch) and flint for building (Vol.1: 30).

This is the outstanding surviving Norman castle site in Norfolk (*pace* Norwich!). The plan of the castle layout has survived almost complete - a round motte, surrounded by a deep ditch, and the outer bailey within which remains of several buildings show up well as earthworks. Excavations between 1970 and 1985 have shown that the motte evolved from its beginnings as a fortified country house into a full-blown keep. The castle was the centre for the Norfolk estates of William de Warenne, a major supporter of William the Conqueror who was granted many manors in Norfolk in addition to his estates in Sussex based on Lewes Castle. The castle was begun in about 1070 and the great keep completed around 1140.

The town of Castle Acre is a shrunken, planned Norman town. The decay of the castle and the dissolution of the priory in 1537 delivered death blows to its importance, and nearby Swaffham replaced it as a market. The town was defended by a massive ditch on its south, west and north sides, and strong gates to north and south. The north ditch has been infilled and become the site of a later green surrounded by attractive buildings. The town has one surviving gate and a number of seventeenth- and eighteenth-century houses which show evidence of the robbing of stone from castle and priory.

Beyond the town ditch lies the parish church of St James, a largely perpendicular church dating from the fourteenth and fifteenth centuries. West of the churchyard is the boundary wall and lane of the priory precinct. The priory lies to the west of that wall off the picture (45).

Medieval castles

44 Caister Castle

TG 504 122 Open

Sir John Fastolf (c.1378-1459), the builder of Caister Castle, was born in the manor house, which may have been situated in the moated base court at the top of the picture, which has brick walls of possibly late fourteenth-century date. Fastolf began his castle, which is also of brick, in 1432. As well as being a symbol of Fastolf's wealth and power, the castle was probably intended to be a strong-point against raids from France and the Low Countries. Bricks were brought from a brickfield about 2.5km due south along a cut or fleet, Pickerell's Fleet, the end of which is just visible passing under an arch (bottom right hand corner). The drum tower standing by this arch may have been the earliest part of Fastolf's building. The bricks were unloaded in the barge-yard immediately north east of this tower.

The castle is dominated by the 90ft (27m) five-storey tower overlooking the landscape and the upper court, which had buildings on all four sides. The main entrance to the castle was over the bridge (top left), into the base court, and over a cross-moat, now filled in, that separated the two courts. Fastolf's inventory of 1459 names three halls, twenty-six chambers, and domestic offices, but the arrangement of the rooms is not known, and the outlines of the walls marked out on the grass in concrete quite recently are modern approximations. The long building with chimneystacks, attached to the drum tower, is the Georgian Caister Hall, and the building with shallow-pitched roofs is the museum. Fastolf intended to found a college of priests at Caister, but his intention was not carried out, and the castle passed to the Paston family. The Duke of Norfolk laid claim to it, and in 1469, after a month's siege, forced its surrender. After his death in 1476 the Pastons regained it, and it remained in their possession until 1659, when Sir William Paston sold it. Sometime after this most of the castle was demolished, and by about 1725 it had been reduced to its present state.

Castle Acre Priory

Medieval monasteries

45

TF 814 818 Open

This splendid photograph shows the ruins of the Cluniac priory at Castle Acre, founded in the afterglow of a visit to Cluny Abbey in Burgundy by William de Warenne and his wife, Gundrada. Even in ruins the house is of considerable architectural splendour. In about 1090 building was begun close to the castle, but the site proved too cramped and this low-lying meadow beside the River Nar was selected by the prior and William de Warenne II.

The quire (low centre right) was begun at the end of the eleventh century and the whole complex around the 100ft (30.5m) square cloister was complete by the mid-twelfth century. The original church had five apses at the east end and the chapter house was also apsidal. Extensive rebuilding in the fourteenth and fifteenth centuries removed all these apses except that of the south transept chapel, but the curved outlines of the apses to the chapter house and quire can be seen here.

From the River Nar (just visible bottom left) a cut was made to bring water to the site. The water entered at the bottom of the picture (right centre) and flowed through the magnificent twelve-seater reredorter or privy, the fifteenth-century kitchen lying astride the drain, and the little water-mill beyond. A separate sewer passed through the south side of the building in a deep-walled drain. The most complete buildings are the sixteenth-century prior's lodgings and the two porches to the guest-house which retain their roofs and were lived in until the nineteenth century.

The outer court on the far left (excavated in the 1970s) consisted of a long barn beside the drain, a grain-dryer and a malthouse, bakehouse and brewhouse with remains of three vats.

Medieval monasteries

46 Thetford Priory

TL 866 833 Open

This Cluniac priory was originally founded by Roger Bigod in 1103-4 on the site previously occupied by the early cathedral for the diocese of East Anglia before it was moved to Norwich. In 1107 the priory moved to this spacious position on the then western edge of the town, with Bigod laying the foundation stone. The building was finished by 1114. There were subsequent alterations to the site, one of these being the result of events in the early twelfth century: a man with an allegedly incurable disease was visited three times by Our Lady and told to ask for a Lady Chapel north of the church. The prior built a wooden chapel but the Virgin wanted a stone building and after a sequence of further appearances, this was accomplished.

The main building in the centre of the photograph shows the aisled church with its north and south transepts, the Lady Chapel and extended east end. The cloister is prominent nearer the camera. To the left of the main buildings is a two-storied prior's lodge, heavily altered in post-medieval times. In the lower right-hand corner is the unusual infirmary or hospital grouped around its own cloister.

The fourteenth-century gatehouse is visible at the top of the photograph. To its left are former farm buildings, the two nearest having medieval timber frames. One has been identified as a court house or granary with accommodation, the other a probable guest hall. Both are considered unique examples of buildings of this type surviving from parts of the monastic inner court.

Despite the efforts of Howard, Duke of Norfolk, to save it, the priory was dissolved in 1539.

Little Walsingham Priory

Medieval monasteries

47

TF 935 367 Open

The Augustinian priory of canons was founded at Little Walsingham in the mid twelfth century. Some years before, the Lady of the Manor, Richeldis de Favarches, had a dream in which the Virgin Mary asked her to build a chapel here; it was to be a replica of the House of the Annunciation in Nazareth.

The parch-marks in the centre of the photograph represent the priory church, its walls and pier bases for the aisles, with the masonry of part of the east end still standing. The original chapel lay just to the north of these marks. South of the church was the cloister, on the west side of which was the cellarer's range and guest accommodation above. To the east was the treasury, common room and chapter house, the buttressed outline of which is particularly clear in the picture. On the south side of the cloister was the refectory, and to the south and south east of the priory were the prior's private apartments. One of these rooms survives within Abbey House (centre of photo). There was also a hospital, a chapel and holy wells; the Shirehall, fronting onto the Market Place, is thought to have been a pilgrims' refectory.

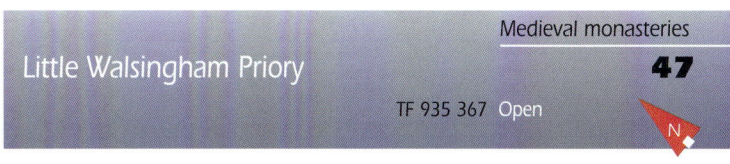

In medieval times the shrine of the Virgin Mary became a focus of pilgrim routes from all directions, including London, and the name 'Walsingham Way' can be found on many old maps. Going on a pilgrimage lessened your time in purgatory, and this shrine also had relics and waters with curative properties. The great European scholar Erasmus visited it in 1511, and Catherine of Aragon and Henry VIII frequented the shrine, the latter paying for a priest and for a candle to be kept burning there, but its popularity ensured its thorough destruction during the Dissolution.

In 1922 a new statue of the Virgin set up in the parish church initiated a revival in the pilgrimages, and the new shrine (top left) was built in the 1930s.

Medieval monasteries

48 St Benet's Abbey, Horning

TG 382 156 Open

St Benet's, or St Benedict's, Abbey occupied an area of rising ground called Cow Holm, an island of dry land in the marshes beside the river Bure. The abbey's origins are shrouded in mystery. Some traditions suggest a Middle Saxon date but it was probably founded in later Saxon times by King Cnut. By the time of the Norman Conquest it had extensive possessions in north-east Norfolk, which were considerably augmented over subsequent centuries.

The curious feature in the foreground of the photograph is the gatehouse, built soon after 1327, which has a later drainage mill erected somewhat incongruously within it - a scene immortalised in countless sketches, paintings and photographs. The remains of the wall surrounding the abbey, which was erected around the same time as the gatehouse, are picked out by a line of thorn bushes. The scanty remains of the abbey church, on the highest point of the 'island', can be seen (Vol.1: 36). It was a building of some pretensions - 100m long and up to 30m wide, without aisles but flanked on both sides by chapels. Close to the gatehouse is an elaborate series of ponds, used to keep fish caught in the local waterways prior to consumption or sale. Other fish-ponds can be seen on the far side of the island.

The abbey ceased to exist when Henry VIII suppressed all English monasteries in 1539. Uniquely, the abbacy was not technically 'dissolved' but was instead combined with the Bishopric of Norwich. The church and other buildings had been 'utterly ruinated and wasted' before 1585. The abbot's lodgings, close to the river, survived into the nineteenth century as a waterfront inn called the Chequers. The drainage mill within the gatehouse - one of the oldest in Broadland - was built in the 1740s.

Marham Abbey

Medieval monasteries

TF 707 098

The earthworks of the abbey lie to the west of Marham village street which runs across the top of the photograph. The south wall of the nave of the abbey church survives as upstanding masonry in the shadowy garden of the large private house.

The cloister can be seen as a flat rectangular area surrounded by building outlines to the right of the garden. Parts of these appear to overlap a corner of a near-rectangular ditched enclosure in the foreground, possibly predating the abbey. Internal fish-ponds and an outlet channel to the left are visible too.

Two building outlines are obvious in the foreground; the larger of these is a U-shaped complex with an enclosing wall on its fourth side and may have been the abbey infirmary or hospital. A smaller building, of unknown purpose, is also clear to the right.

Marham Abbey was a unique foundation for Cistercian nuns started in 1249 by Isabella, Countess of Arundel, who endowed it with lands and services in Marham. In 1251 the nuns were allowed to have burials, masses and divine services conducted by their own priest in their own church, excluding parishoners of Marham. Never wealthy, it was valued at about £39 in 1535, and at the Dissolution a few years later there were an abbess and eight nuns.

The site is considered to be among the best preserved of the smaller monastic houses in Norfolk and is of special interest as the only Cistercian house in the county.

Medieval monasteries

50 Shouldham Priory

TF 680 095

The priory, Norfolk's only Gilbertine foundation for men and women, was founded after 1193 by Geoffrey FitzPiers, Earl of Essex, during the reign of Richard I. The order, being dual, had separate buildings for men and women, the church being a possible exception. The foundation charter granted the manor of Shouldham and the two parish churches to the monastery. In 1392 the priory was valued at 200 marks (about £133) but had suffered losses by fire, a great gale, and river and sea floods which had destroyed some possessions. At its surrender in 1538 there were a prior, sub-prior, eight canons and a prioress, sub-prioress and five nuns.

Nothing of the priory now survives above ground, the remnants being cleared in 1831, leaving only crop-marks.

Abbey Farm overlies part of the priory buildings, probably the portion reserved for the canons, and to its east can be seen the rectangular east end of the church divided into separate aisles for men and women. A rectangular chapel is visible on the north side. To the north again are the outlines of part of a cloister and the eastern range once occupied by the nuns.

On lower ground to the north and north-east of the site are two curving parallel crop-marks representing an elaborate system of sanitation and water management. The southern one took drainage and supplied water for fish-ponds and tanks, and the northern one fed the nearby group of fish-ponds clearly visible in the foreground.

Some earthworks lie in the area between the farm and the village; although of uncertain nature, they appear to be associated with the priory.

Crop-marks of the original Coxford Priory, East Rudham
Medieval monasteries
TF 829 283

The crop-mark of a sizable cruciform church came to light in a field near East Rudham village in 1992. It almost certainly represents the original site of the Augustinian priory founded by William Cheney during the reign of Stephen (1135-54). For reasons which remain obscure, the whole priory was moved to a new site at the eastern boundary of the parish in the thirteenth century (52). This aerial photograph could therefore be of the twelfth century priory church which can only have been in use for about half a century (if, indeed, it was ever completed; the crop-marks, after all, only indicate foundations). No doubt all above-ground materials would have been re-used at the new site.

There is no clear evidence in the photograph of the claustral buildings (cloisters, dormitory, refectory etc) which the Augustinian canons would have used. The rest of the canons' buildings may have been made of flimsier materials such as wood, with the intention of building in stone at a later date.

Construction of the church must have been the priority. Its outline is clear enough. An apsidal choir with crossing, transepts and an aisleless nave. An apse, rather than a square east end, would have been rare after *c.*1150. A date not long after 1135 therefore seems likely.

Medieval monasteries

52 Coxford Priory, East Rudham

TF 848 290

Upstanding fragments of Coxford Priory are limited to the scanty remains of the nave and chancel of the church, but outlines of other buildings are obvious in this picture as parch marks in the grass. Parts of two wings of the cloister are just visible in the wooded and disturbed area nearer the camera. Other building outlines can be seen nearby within a partly-moated inner court, while outside it, to the lower left, are parts of a system of monastic fish-ponds. Beyond the moat a west-to-east range of buildings is clearly visible; to the left vegetation conceals another range which runs north to south.

This Augustinian priory was founded about 1140. Initially near East Rudham village (51), it was moved eastwards to Coxford when William de Cheney, lord of Rudham, gave the priory a new site. His charter mentioned a mill, a fish-pond, Caldewellwang and the land between it and the water of Tattersett, Ketellesmerewang and Noremerewang. Caldewellwang ('field or enclosure with a cold spring') probably refers to a field, behind the camera, where there is an active spring.

The priory received many benefactions and when dissolved in 1534 was valued at over £121. There were then a prior and nine canons.

Eccles church, Lessingham

Medieval churches

53

TG 414 288 Open

During the early seventeenth century the low lying east Norfolk coastal village of Eccles was inundated by the North Sea. Considered during medieval times as a 'good fishing town', Eccles was devastated; a petition by its remaining inhabitants to the Norwich Sessions in 1643 for a reduction of taxes, stated that only 100 acres of the parish's 2000 acres remained and that 'they are daily wasting'. The medieval church of St Mary's lay in ruins with only its round tower left standing. Although protected by sand-hills during the next two centuries, this too eventually succumbed to the sea in the fierce storm of 23 January 1895.

This photograph was taken on 29 April 1991, twelve days after spring tides and a strong north-westerly wind caused one of the most spectacular beach scours at Eccles this century. Large sections of flint masonry - once part of St Mary's nave, chancel and south aisle walls - lay uncovered, rolled by the tides from their original positions. Only a single, semi-circular section of tower remained *in situ*, with three other large pieces thrown over towards the sea in a northerly direction. The dark area extending from the church ruins towards the sea wall (at the top of the picture) is part of the churchyard where the remains of many skeletons were exposed, a few still lying within trapezium-shaped coffins. Just below the sea wall on the other side of the wooden groyne lay a circular, clay-lined well, one of ten medieval wells exposed near the precincts of the church.

An area scoured free of sand immediately east of the churchyard (just off the picture) yielded many pieces of medieval pottery and was intersected by a number of ancient paths and roadways, some still retaining the remnants of their original cobble surfaces.

Medieval churches

54 Islington church, Tilney All Saints

TF 570 168 Open

The ruins of St Mary the Virgin, Islington, stand prominently beside a roundabout on the busy A47. It is hard now to picture the scene earlier this century when the church stood deep in the park of Islington Hall. The hall itself, now equally exposed, lies just to the east of the church, but out of the photograph. The church was in use until after the Second World War, but was then abandoned to vandals and, more disastrously, to thieves who stripped the lead from the roof. This resulted in the collapse of the nave roof and with it a coved plaster ceiling dating from the late eighteenth or early nineteenth century. At this point it was made into a safe ruin. The wall monuments were assembled in the chancel, which remains roofed, and are visible through a grille at the chancel arch.

The main structure of the church seems to date from late in the thirteenth century. The transepts are deep and make one wonder whether nave aisles were intended but never realised. The tower is sturdy, although not ill-proportioned, and seems to be a new build of about 1450. It is carstone rag as far as the belfry stage and then red brick. The north porch, in its present form, followed.

In the Domesday Survey Islington was the second wealthiest of these Marshland vills - West Walton taking first place. But there wasn't the subsequent growth here that the neighbouring parishes knew, and that showed itself in their flashy churches. Islington remained modest, and what settlement there was drifted away to the south, leaving the church abandoned.

Heckingham church

Medieval churches 55

TM 384 988 Open

This simple Norman church, away from any concentration of settlement, is typical of many rural parish churches in Norfolk where the population has migrated elsewhere for economic or other reasons, leaving the church in isolation. Extensive fieldwalking in the parish has revealed much evidence of domestic activity, with pottery sherds, dating from the Middle Saxon period up to the fourteenth century, found in the fields surrounding the church. To the left of the picture is a farmhouse situated within a moat. Documentary research shows that the hall of the Buckmongers estate stood here in 1562.

The church of St Gregory is a fine example of a Norman church, dating from about 1140, to judge from the exceptional Romanesque sculpture on the south door. This belongs to a group of doorways in south-east Norfolk related to Norwich Cathedral through the common use of distinctive carving. The western tower retains the lower part of the original round tower, the upper part of which was replaced in the fifteenth century, probably following a collapse, with an octagonal structure with brick quoins. Round western towers were the rule in twelfth-century Norfolk. The originally aisleless nave and chancel of St Gregory's are thatched with reed. The chancel is slightly narrower than the nave and is special in having retained its apsidal east end. Other surviving apsidal chancels in the county are nearby at Hales and Fritton but the apse is a characteristic of Romanesque architecture and almost every twelfth-century parish church chancel had one. In the late thirteenth century a north aisle was added to the nave and a rough arcade was formed by cutting through the north wall. The south porch was added during the fifteenth century.

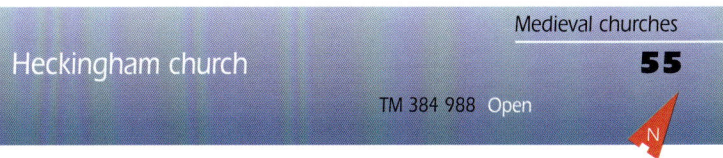

Medieval churches

56 Church of St Michael and all Angels, Booton
TG 123 224 Open

The building now visible in all its wonderful eccentricity was designed by the Rev. Whitwell Elwin who lived at Booton from 1849-1900.

The original church on this site consisted of a west tower, nave and chancel and Elwin's new creation, built between 1876 and 1900, followed these lines, encasing the original building within its walls and adding a large baptistry at the west and a vestry on the south. Using mainly limestone from Bath and black knapped flint from Mundesley beach, Elwin created new elevations which were dramatic and ornate, with pinnacles on gables and buttresses, and two narrow towers set diagonally to the main structure at the west end with a tall 'minaret' between them. These features appear as a startling landmark rising unexpectedly out of the wide open Norfolk landscape.

Elwin incorporated into his building aspects of other English churches which appealed to him, such as the designs of windows from Temple Balsall, the chapel of St Stephen, Westminster and Lichfield, the design of a porch (from Burgh-next-Aylsham) and a hammer-beam (from Trunch).

The interior echoes the exuberance of the exterior. The hammer-beam roof carries enormous angels with upswept wings, designed to hold lamps, carved by James Minns, who made figureheads for ships. The windows are a riot (though in pleasing colours) of stained glass, the earliest dating to about 1880. The chancel windows depict angel themes from the bible, while the south nave windows have a procession of angelic-looking musicians and the north nave windows female saints and attendant angels, all heading eastwards.

The three small linked buildings near the east end of the church are stables with a harness room between them, presumably for visiting parishioners.

Hilgay is a former island on the eastern edge of Fenland. This complicated site is marked 'Manorial Earthworks' on the Ordnance Survey map, and some of these earthworks are rather unusual. They lie about half a mile north-east of the church to the north of a lane visible in the photograph and bordering Hilgay Fen to the right.

The major feature is a large moated enclosure in the background. The moat is partly water-filled with no convincing original entrance and with some widening and infilling apparent.

Closer to the camera are two very small moated platforms. The most complete of these is irregular with an entrance on the far side; the other is incomplete. Between these and the larger moat are two roughly parallel depressions, and nearest the camera is a large bar-shaped water feature. These may all be fish-ponds, although it is all too easy to call a depression you don't understand a fish-pond.

There are no obvious signs of buildings on the site but any there could have been of timber. The narrower features

Medieval countryside

Hilgay moats and fish-ponds

57

TL 625 986

running back from the lane are obviously modern drainage ditches, although this is still a very wet field and it is likely that the buried, waterlogged archaeology could be very well-preserved.

A list of landholders dated 1316 notes the Abbey of Ramsey, the Abbey of St Edmundsbury and Earl Warenne as all having lands here. So which manorial site these features represent is not clear.

Medieval countryside

58 Bixley deserted medieval village

TG 258 049

The site of the deserted village of Bixley lies only 3km south of Norwich; apart from the church of St Wandregeselius, all that survives are very well-preserved earthworks in these four fields. There are three north to south roadways (left to right in the picture) running across the site. One, visible as a double hedgerow nearest the camera, was still in use in 1797 as the main Norwich to Bungay road, but the other two, interlinked and appearing as irregular linear hollow ways, became disused in earlier times.

Groups of tofts, or house sites, outlined by rectangular banks or ditches, are scattered over the site. One group lies on either side of the most distant roadway, where the earthworks are especially clear.

It is a pity that documentary evidence for this, the best-preserved deserted medieval village site in eastern Norfolk, is so sparse. In 1086 the record shows quite a substantial population with a church, yet by 1334 its tax payments were the lowest in the district. Thereafter it appears to have dwindled gradually. By 1603 there were still twenty-five communicants (people over sixteen years of age) and in 1664 the Hearth Tax was levied on twenty-nine hearths but fifteen of them belonged to Sir Edward Ward at Bixley Hall, well to the south of the village. The village therefore appears to have declined over several centuries and was largely deserted by the sixteenth century.

The dedication to St Wandregeselius, Abbot of Fontanelle in seventh-century Normandy, is unique in England.

Rougham deserted medieval village

Medieval countryside

TF 825 206

Rougham was a very large village in early medieval times but had undergone severe economic decline by the 1500s. In 1349, the year of the Black Death, the main landowner was John Reed. He had a reputation as a grasping man of wealth, being not only a collector of taxes, including the Poll Tax, but also a creditor and debtor. He was targeted by insurgent peasants, including many from Rougham, at the time of the Peasants' Revolt in 1381. After this he continued to enlarge his own lands, probably including the area in the photograph. A document of 1511 describes pastures which appear to include the surviving earthworks, shown in the picture. So the village was presumably deserted by the early sixteenth century, if not before.

To the right a disused roadway, once known as Hildemere or Lynn Way, is clearly visible extending towards the modern village at the top of the photograph. Another, Massingham Gate or Overgate (from the Old Norse 'gata', meaning a road or street), emerges from the plantation on the left and appears to be joining it. Between are a number of tofts or house sites and banked enclosures partly disfigured by more recent pits. No significant pottery later than about 1400 has been found in the area, and it is a delight that such an extensive area of the medieval village earthworks has survived, although ploughing has removed the earthworks on the right. Hidden by trees to the left are the impressive remains of eighteenth- and nineteenth-century estate brickworks.

Medieval countryside

60 Gayton manorial earthworks

TF 719 195

These earthworks lie in three fields to the west of Gayton village alongside the King's Lynn road. Most prominent is a curving ditch clearly visible to the right of the road. This was the edge of a former common. The central field contains the most important features. Here a short hollow way, or abandoned roadway, leads from the former common into a complicated group of earthworks and enclosures which may well have contained manorial buildings.

A map of 1726 marks this as the likely site of West Hall Manor, but by then all the buildings had disappeared. One of the fields was called West Hall Close; another was West Hall Bushey Close. Otherwise documents tell us little about the site.

In the right hand part of the central field the remains of ridge and furrow, surviving from medieval fields, are just visible. It is extremely unusual in Norfolk to find earthworks of medieval settlement and fields preserved together in the same field. (Examples of ridge and furrow alone can be seen in **65** and **66**.)

Waterden deserted medieval village, South Creake

Medieval countryside

TF 886 362

Waterden lay in a shallow valley occupied by a small stream draining southwards toward the bottom of the picture. Only the eastern part of the site in the right of the photograph survives as earthworks; the western portion was levelled in around 1966, but it still showed as soil colours when this picture was taken in 1976. The main street can be seen as a linear sunken way to the right of the ponds. Pond-digging has disfigured the site of a village green which is shown intact on a map of 1713. To the right of the green at this date there were about six house sites. On the other side there appear to have been three more houses as well as an enclosure for a Hall built in around 1600.

A medieval village of modest prosperity in 1334, Waterden had suffered severe economic decline by 1449. By 1603 there were only twenty communicants (people over sixteen years of age). The manor was purchased in 1483 by the Sefoules who held it until the end of the sixteenth century when they sold it to Sir Edward Coke, and it has remained part of the Holkham estate since. It seems likely that the remnants of medieval Waterden disappeared at about this time.

Waterden Farm, part of which appears on the photograph, was completed in 1784, but an older barn of about 1600 survives among the farm buildings (Vol.1: 76).

Medieval countryside

62 New Buckenham Common

TM 091 907 Open

New Buckenham common is part of a landscape largely created by the d'Albini barons, owners of the Buckenham estate from the late eleventh century. On the right of the photograph a wide ditch interrupted by nineteenth- and twentieth-century farm buildings marks the southern boundary of their great hunting park. The gently curving hedge that bisects the straight lane in the top left-hand corner follows the boundary ditch of the Haugh, an oval enclosure, possibly a detached deer park, belonging to the bishop's manor of Eccles. At the top of the photograph is the borough, laid out in a grid pattern at his new castle gates (just out of the picture at top right) by the first Earl William d'Albini between about 1150 and 1176 (Vol.1: 32). Use of the common was confirmed to the burgesses by the second Earl William in a charter dated between 1176 and 1193. Other features include the beck across the common, which fed the town ditch, and the castle moat and ditches which must represent attempts to drain the wet common soil. An irregular central enclosure surrounds the site of a windmill; it is now a car repair garage.

Bisecting the common, the straight road was built under a Turnpike Act of 1772 and the scar of its slightly more erratic predecessor is seen below it. The many shallow depressions, some dry, some water-filled and some scrub-grown, are the result of flint, sand and clay digging recorded in the 1590s and later. Below the mill enclosure is Spittlemere, documented in 1635 and probably formed from flooded mineral workings. The tree-lined causeway of an old road to Tibenham marks the common's farther boundary. At the right-hand corner, the triangle cut off by a curving road had developed as an external town green by the 1560s when a 'gameplace' is recorded there. It is now a play area and cricket ground.

Brisley Green

Medieval countryside

63

TF 955 208 Open

Brisley Green, covering an area of 52ha, is an excellent example of a surviving medieval common. It lies on the boulder clay plateau of north Norfolk in an area bounded on the north, east and south by the valley of the River Wensum and those of its tributaries. The view is looking north from the southern end of the common, and the B1145 Bawdeswell to Litcham road crosses the middle of the common.

The sweeping lines of multi-species hedges are typical of the ditches and hedged boundaries which define such commons. The farms lying on the edge of the common are also a further characteristic. Clay pits are scattered along the edges of the common, and these would have provided water for stock and clay or gravel for building purposes. It has been suggested that the large area on the east side of the photograph and a smaller area north of the main road were relatively late enclosures into the common. It is possible that much of the common is the remnant shape of earlier woodland abutting Panford Beck (out of picture, to the right) when Burgrave Wood in North Elmham abutted Brisley.

The common would probably have been 'stinted', i.e. limited as to the number of stock it carried, originally cattle rather than sheep. Parishioners would have cut timber, furze and possibly turf from it, even peat, by Panford Beck. A small rectangle at the south end of the common may be a former hall site or perhaps the pound where stock could be penned in. Since most commons were enclosed in the late eighteenth and early nineteenth centuries, why there was no parliamentary enclosure act for Brisley is an interesting question.

Medieval countryside

64 Hockering Park - looking north-east

TG 085 135

The outline formed in this picture by hedgerows has survived in the landscape for four hundred, perhaps six hundred, years. In 1581 Lord Morley is recorded as having a park in Hockering and earlier, in 1317, Sir John Marshall held one too, but it is not certain if it was the same one. The sweeping lines of a ring fence and ditch against which boundaries inside and outside are discontinuous often reflect the existence of a former deer park. The present name of Park Farm on modern maps and on Bryant's map of 1826 is also revealing: however, neither the Tithe Map of 1839 nor Faden's map of 1797 name it. This shows how difficult it can be to establish longevity and continuity of a place name.

Perhaps surprisingly, the left, western boundary of the park oversteps the line of the small stream which flows southwards off the clay plateau to the valley of the River Tud. The southern and northern boundaries of the park form sweeping curves but the eastern boundary is less regular and follows the parish boundary between Hockering and Honingham. Unusually for Norfolk it would seem that a manorial boundary was also a parish boundary.

The boundary ditch and hedge of such parks were to prevent the deer escaping. Park Farmhouse may have originated as the park keeper's dwelling. Henry Saynt John was keeper of the park in 1581. The crop-mark of a moated site south-west of Park Farm may reveal the site of an earlier park keeper's house. By 1839 it was a ring-fenced farm and the large fields to the north-east of the farmhouse were called Home Pastures, suggesting that it was still grazing land, but for cattle rather than deer.

Stradsett ridge and furrow

Medieval countryside

65

TF 666 055

The photograph shows part of one of the largest surviving areas of medieval cultivation strips in Norfolk. These are preserved as slightly curving, near parallel ridges in grassland within and to the west of Stradsett Park, straddling the A134. The strips are between 5 and 9m wide, and no more than 0.3m high. They were individually cultivated, mostly with horses in Norfolk, with tenants usually holding several strips throughout the 'open fields' of the parish. The furrows formed a boundary between the strips as well as providing drainage. Their preservation as earthworks is due to the land being turned over to sheep pasture after enclosure when arable cultivation ceased.

The existence of these features in Norfolk is rare compared with many Midland and Northern counties, and is confined almost entirely to a narrow belt in the west of the county, around the fen edges from Babingley in the north to Hilgay in the south (**66**).

The photograph also shows other aspects of the landscape history of the park. Part of an earlier drive to the hall can be seen to the right running under the tennis courts. The light rectangular patch, central to the photograph, is a former cricket square.

Medieval countryside

66 Hilgay ridge and furrow

TF 666 055

This photograph of February 1989, looking south, shows ridge and furrow strikingly enhanced by waterlogged hollows. The area surrounding Lodge Farm at the southern end of Hilgay was one of the best surviving examples of ridge and furrow in Norfolk until it was ploughed in 1991. At least twenty-six strip fields can be counted running parallel to each other. Two later ditches, one straight and the other curved, have been dug across the line of the old field system. In the field beyond, blocks of ridge and furrow, which run in two different orientations, are visible.

Fortunately, the area in the immediate foreground still survives, as part of an extensive layout of strips on the gentle south- and west-facing slope between the village and the by-pass road.

Middleton Towers

TF 668 175

Great houses 67

The gatehouse of Middleton Towers is a fine piece of fifteenth-century brickwork with elaborate octagonal towers in each corner. It was probably started by the seventh Lord Scales who was killed in 1460, so it is just earlier than Oxborough. The building work was continued by Scales' successors, although little more than the west wing (left in the picture) was built. The moat dates from this period.

How long the house was ever occupied is not clear. Engravings of the gatehouse in the late eighteenth and early nineteenth centuries show the gatehouse roofless, the windows broken and in poor repair, and only fragments of the west wing standing above ground. The moat was by then hardly visible and largely infilled.

The place underwent a major refurbishment after it was bought by Sir Lewis Whincop Jarvis in 1856. The gatehouse was repaired and the west wing entirely rebuilt by 1864. The embattled corner tower was finished in 1876. Thereafter the wing which runs north from the corner tower was added by the Ramsden family. As a part of this refurbishment the moat was cleaned out leaving a glimpse of what might have been had the original building work continued.

Great houses

68 Oxburgh Hall

TF 742 012 Open

Oxburgh Hall, one of the most romantic of moated houses, was built in 1480 by Sir Edmund Bedingfeld on receipt of a 'licence to crenellate' from Edward IV, following his family's support of the Yorkist cause in the Wars of the Roses (Vol.1: 61). Steadfastly Catholic in the centuries which followed Henry VIII's schism with Rome, the Bedingfelds were denied both station and preferment by the crown. If things had been otherwise, and income from high office had flowed into Oxburgh's coffers, perhaps less of the hall's late fifteenth-century fabric would have survived to be enjoyed today.

1829 was a significant year for Oxburgh's fortunes: not only was The Act of Catholic Emancipation passed, but Henry Bedingfeld, recently married to an heiress from Norfolk's ancient Paston family, succeeded his father as 6th Baronet. In addition to restoring and remodelling the hall during the following thirty years with the assistance of the architect John Chessell Buckler, Henry Bedingfeld built the Roman Catholic chapel (foreground) and laid out the colourful parterre to the north of the Hall. Although undocumented, family tradition maintains that the chapel of 1836 was designed by A. C. Pugin. If so, stylistic evidence suggests it is his earliest ecclesiastical work. The chapel was supposedly constructed from re-used brick taken from demolished cottages in the village. The parterre, laid out in the 1840s, conforms closely to a design illustrated in the early eighteenth-century treatise *La Theorie et la Pratique du Jardinage* by Antoine d'Argenville.

An earlier garden feature is also worth noting. Beyond the south-west corner of the moat (right) lies an area of earthworks. Described on a map of 1722 as 'The Quarters', it appears to have been an early eighteenth-century water garden, subsequently infilled to become raised walkways.

Hunstanton Hall, Old Hunstanton

Great houses

69

TF 692 418

Hunstanton Hall is one of Norfolk's most impressive fortified manor sites and is the architectural symbol of one of Norfolk's oldest estates, that of the Le Strange family. The family held land in Norfolk in the early twelfth century and the estate continued in their hands until the eighteenth century when the Styleman family took the name.

The hall, or manor house, is a building of three main periods. A little classical gateway leads from the park which lies to the east of the house into an outer courtyard bounded on its north side by a long barn. A moat surrounds the house proper and a brick bridge leads to the gatehouse c.1500. Either side of the gatehouse are Jacobean wings faced in a chequer pattern of carstone and Barnack stone. The great hall, lost in a fire in 1853, was replaced by a Victorian extension. A second wider 'moat', or lake, edges the lawns to the west of the hall. The estate's influence on the landscape is emphasised by the planted woods and the handsome parkland trees in the foreground.

The church of St Mary, with an offset square tower, was much restored by Henry Le Strange Styleman Le Strange in 1857. On the northern edge of the photograph the line of the street of Old Hunstanton can just be seen. New Hunstanton, to the west of the area shown, was created by the Le Stranges as an exclusive holiday resort and it was served by the extension of the railway from King's Lynn in 1862.

A distinctive and attractive feature of both Old and New Hunstanton is that many of the buildings are built of, or in part built of, carstone, an orange sandstone that occurs beneath the chalk and which outcrops in the cliffs at Old Hunstanton (11).

Great houses

70 Stiffkey Hall

TF 974 429

Sir Nicholas Bacon, Lord Keeper to Elizabeth I, designed Stiffkey Hall for his second son Nathaniel in 1576. He planned it as a square courtyard house with a turret at each of its outer and inner corners and with terraced gardens (centre of photograph) to its east, descending from the churchyard's southern wall to the flood-plain of the river. House and gardens were planned as a unity, incorporating mathematical ratios commonly adopted by renaissance designers. Nathaniel, lacking his father's vision (and probably the cash), failed to complete the scheme. He never built the south range, which should have stood where two shed-like buildings appear in the photograph; nor, probably because of the quantity of land-fill required, did he complete the eastern terraces which should have extended the full length of the churchyard wall. As a result the gardens lacked the proportions originally planned, and Sir Nicholas's masterstroke of incorporating the churchyard as the final court in a geometric chequer-board scheme was ruined (the wall of a courtyard to the north of the house appears as a white line).

The turrets might suggest a fortified house, but this would have been unlikely in Elizabethan times; rather they may reflect an English vernacular version of French chateau features. Sir Nicholas built three great houses, but their gardens were his passion. In two of them he displayed a fascination for incorporating canals in their layout. At Stiffkey he re-aligned the river to provide a canal-like feature which was bisected by a carriageway and bridge leading to the house (left-hand side of photograph). The mathematics of this house and its gardens demanded a six-acre site on rising ground; to acquire this, Sir Nichols bought up and 'plucked down' houses and barns adjacent to the church, effectively moving the village westward (see top of photograph).

After Nathaniel's death in 1622 the property passed to Sir Roger Townshend who lived here while building Raynham Hall. Thereafter it was occupied by tenant farmers and suffered partial demolition. The house overlooked a magnificent estuary whose flood waters, until blocked by a late medieval sea bank, reached up to Warham and whose reclaimed flood-plain can be seen, now traversed by Bridge Street (top left).

Blickling Hall was built for Sir Henry Hobart (pronounced Hubbard), James I's Lord Chief Justice of the Common Pleas, by the architect Robert Lyminge between the years 1619 and 1626 (Vol.1: 65). Altered little until the second half of the eighteenth century, and then, in a remarkably early antiquarian exercise, with due deference to its powerful Jacobean character, Blickling is amongst the county's most beautiful houses. At a time when its architecture could hardly have been fashionable, the eighteenth-century poetess Hannah More wrote of the putative birthplace of Ann Boleyn: 'You admire Houghton, but you wish for Blickling; you look at Houghton with astonishment, at Blickling with desire'.

Certainly the view of the south front of Blickling Hall, pictured here, remains a breathtaking site as the visitor first encounters it, suddenly and unexpectedly, at right angles to the Aylsham Road. The brick façade with its central clock tower, shaped gables and leaded turrets is made more dramatic by its framing; to either side of the Great Court are projecting service ranges - originally Offices and Stables - their line continued south as far again by a pair of remarkable yew hedges, perhaps nearly as old as the house. The brickwork of the stable range to the east (right) is the earliest identified example of Flemish bond in the country.

Behind the clock tower, rebuilt by John Adey Repton in the early nineteenth century, Blickling's two internal courtyards can be clearly seen. They are separated by a cross-range whose origins pre-date the Jacobean house; Lyminge incorporated part of the fabric of the great hall of the moated Tudor manor house, its size and shape determining its successor. Beyond this the flat leaded roof and windowless south facing wall of the second courtyard identify the late eighteenth-century north range.

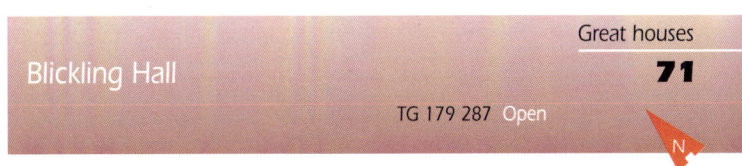

Great houses

Blickling Hall

71

TG 179 287 Open

Great houses

72 Site of the old hall, Rougham

TF 829 206

This complex of parch-marks in Rougham Park marks the site of Rougham Hall, demolished in the late eighteenth century. The hall has an important place in British architectural history. It was built by Roger North, lawyer, historian, and gentleman architect, soon after he purchased the Rougham estate in 1693. North described his activities here in a manuscript - *Cursory Notes of Building* - which remained unpublished in his own lifetime. His account shows that in reality he largely reconstructed and adapted an existing building, in part of medieval origins, giving it a symmetrical elevation and a free-standing Ionic portico - the earliest in eastern England. The hall was an important essay in Palladian architecture, a style which bridges the gap between the seventeenth-century classicism of Inigo Jones and the early eighteenth-century architecture of Lord Burlington, Colen Campbell and their set.

The parch-marks represent features added by North, as well as some which he probably removed (and others, perhaps, which had disappeared before his time). Among other things the old cross-passage running at one end of the hall (changed into an open arcade by North), the west wing of the house, where North's own private rooms were located (to the left), and a variety of ancillary and service rooms to the rear can be seen. In front, traces of the portico are just visible and, to the south of this, the outline of a courtyard enclosed by a low wall (the double line running from right to left).

The hall was set in elaborate gardens, which survive in part as low earthworks. More striking is the avenue of lime trees which extends for some 2km to the south of the hall; and the complex 'fan' of sweet chestnuts, the remains of a wilderness or ornamental wood, ranged either side of this. Both were apparently planted by Roger North. The present Rougham Hall probably originated as a detached service block to the old hall; it was improved and extended at various times in the nineteenth and twentieth centuries.

Houghton Hall

TF 791 287 Open

Great houses 73

Old Houghton Hall, a double-pile house with small interior courtyards, was sited between the projecting wings and immediately to the west of the present mansion. Aligned on the old house was a sixteen-acre (6.5ha) formal garden, completed just before 1720. The presence of this new, expensive garden probably determined Robert Walpole (1676-1745) to choose this site rather than a more elevated one for his new house, designed by Colen Campbell in the neo-Palladian style, with Thomas Ripley as the executant (Vol.1: 66). It was built between 1722 and 1735. Central exterior stairs, which gave access to the first-floor staterooms, were removed c.1780; the present west stairs (not visible here) were built in 1973. Quadrant passages connect the mansion to the South Office (left), containing domestic rooms and fourteen bedrooms, and the North Office, which contained picture gallery, chapel, dairy, laundry, and brewery. This wing was partly gutted by fire in 1791.

The only traces of the 1720 formal garden are the ha-ha on the north side (just visible top right) and a bank between the single tree (top left) and the light double-lozenge figure. The garden was overgrown by 1761, its neglect by Sir Robert's eccentric grandson, the third Earl of Orford (1730-91), being more responsible than any change of taste. The light outlines in the grass are the 25ft (7.6m) wide gravel paths of the garden layout of c.1850, which existed until after 1900. The trapezium shape, the far side measuring 210ft (64m), enclosed round and quadrant beds, and there were beds, shrubs, and clipped cupolar bushes of box, privet, and yew to each side and beyond the cross-path. Gravel paths in the shape of two lozenges with anthemion-patterned beds, joined by a circle surrounded by a pergola and a fleur-de-lys pattern on either side, completed the layout. The small trees to the right were planted about 1949.

Great houses

74 Houghton Hall walled garden and stables

TF 789 285 Open

The old village of Houghton was demolished in the 1730s and replaced by New Houghton (**Vol.1: 67**), over half a mile south of the new mansion built by Sir Robert Walpole. The old village street ran to the north of the church and pond (centre top) and divided, on the site of the quadrangular stables (left) into roads heading for Anmer, Flitcham and Harpley, all closed in the late 1720s. The stables, built between 1733 and 1736, replaced others of 1721 that blocked the south view from the new house. The site of the demolished stables was turned into an oval pond, the southern half of which is visible as a slight depression beyond the new stables. These are of brick, faced on the outside with carstone except on the lower part of the west and south walls, where the removal of lean-tos left brickwork exposed.

The original walled kitchen garden extended northwards along the west wall of the stables, but between 1800 and 1826 it was reduced to its present size and a new north wall built. The five-acre (2ha) garden, which in about 1950 was neat and well-ordered, had become run-down by 1991, when Lord Cholmondeley began a programme of renovation. The design of the formal parterre garden (top left-hand quarter) is based on the ceiling of the White Drawing Room in the mansion, while the top right-hand quarter is a 'wilderness' and the bottom right-hand quarter an orchard. To the right of the garden the Carpenters' Yard Barn, now converted to estate workshops, was probably built around 1730 as the foxhounds' kennel. The building in the foreground contains a remnant of a pre-1720 tumbled gable, but its stepped gables, double-headed gothick windows, and much of the front wall date from the 1840s.

Holkham Hall

Great houses

TF 884 428 Open

Holkham Hall, built between 1734 and 1764 for Thomas Coke, remains the home of his descendants, the Earls of Leicester, and of the magnificent art treasures collected on his Grand Tour, when, for nearly six years from 1712 to 1718, he travelled and studied in France, Italy, Germany and the Low Countries. The central block contains the state rooms; the wings accommodated 'Family', 'Strangers', 'Chapel', and 'Kitchen'. The classical symmetry of the hall, and its hard white brick, give an impression of unchanging permanence. No trace remains of the village which occupied the site when Coke decided to build, or of the manor house, in Coke's family since 1612, which for some years was linked to the first wing of the hall (lower left in the photograph).

Work on laying out the grounds began some years before the hall (**Vol.1: 69**). To the west, a marshy depression was excavated to form the lake; the curves at both ends were added in later years. To the south, William Kent designed a formal basin, flanked by ornamental pavilions, and beyond it straight lines of trees leading due south across a great lawn. This stage has disappeared as completely as the original village: the terraces, parterres and fountain all date from the mid nineteenth century, as does the cricket pitch to the north of the hall. Around the same period, new buildings transformed the aspect to the east: nearest the house are the laundry (now the Holkham Pottery) and the conservatory (now without its iron roof); on the extreme right are the stables (now the restaurant and Bygones collection). The roof of the octagonal game larder indicates the only survivor of the earlier domestic offices. Just out of the photograph is the estate office, still the centre of the large agricultural estate founded 400 years ago by Lord Chief Justice Coke.

Great houses

76 Dunston Hall before reconstruction

TG 225 020

Dunston Hall seen in early 1990 is a Victorian country house in crisis, shorn of its land and with agriculture and forestry advancing towards the main block over the derelict park and gardens. In the Long family since 1654, the estate passed to Kellet cousins in 1797. Robert Kellet Long took over the estate in 1836 and spent a fortune in an unsuccessful battle to keep the new railway to Norwich away from his country seat. The new house was thus born into adversity. Built in red brick in 1859, to a neo-Elizabethan design by Buckler, its high gables, pinnacles and chimneys recall Heydon and Barningham Halls and long-lost Oxnead. Robert died in 1874 and was succeeded by the unfortunate Fortescue Walter Kellet Long, who was detained as of unsound mind in a private asylum in 1877, and lived until 1934. The 3,500-acre (1,400ha) estate was administered by the Court of Chancery and managed by his younger brothers, Charles and Ernest. The house was let on long leases to members of the Lacon and Buxton families. The Long family divided and sold the estate in 1957 and the house was used for a time as a furniture store. By 1977, when it was re-sold to Jimmy (Loyne) Englesen for an ill-fated charitable venture to support disabled performers and musicians, lead thieves, vandals and vermin had reduced the house, still then without mains services, to a pitiful state. Another new owner in 1985 barely stemmed the tide of deterioration and although the integrity of the main block was preserved, the out-buildings were sadly decayed. The laundry, kitchen and kitchen garden can be seen to the left. The billiard room, one of the few changes made to the original house and added in 1881, is to the right.

Dunston Hall after reconstruction

TG 225 020 Open

Great houses

The transformation by the Shaw family, new owners of redundant Dunston Hall, into a hotel, golf and country club, began in January 1991. The facilities opened in 1995, the year of the photograph. Seen from the garden front (the previous view is from the opposite side) the scale of the extensions is clear. The design by MWP Architects Ltd of Lowestoft employs red brick matched in colour and size to that in the original house, and the new gables, roofs and windows reflect its style. The bulk of the new buildings is less apparent from ground level where the superior height of the Victorian block allows it to dominate the complex. On the site of the old garden to the left, the additions embrace the existing billiard room, converted into a function room, and also at ground level a carvery. On the first floor are conference and banqueting suites continuing through the original block. Balancing the old billiard room a single-storey reception wing projects from the other end of the entrance front with a restaurant behind it. Further to the right a bedroom block covers the site of the nineteenth-century domestic wing and kitchen garden.

Below the house at the level of the old cellars are a swimming pool and gymnasium. Beyond the buildings the car parks and leisure pursuits have replaced agriculture, with floodlit tennis courts to the right. The contraction of the area of land associated with the house has been reversed, re-purchases allowing the extension of the golf course to eighteen holes by 1998, covering 52.6ha, with the club house in converted farm buildings.

Great houses

78 Sandringham House

TF 694 287 Open

The Sandringham estate was bought in 1862 for £220,000 by HRH Prince of Wales, the future King Edward VII. A relatively modest white-stuccoed eighteenth-century house was replaced in 1870 with Albert Jenkins Humbert's neo-Jacobean design in brick with Ketton stone dressings (**Vol.1: 73**). Of the earlier house only an extravagantly-decorated conservatory of c.1854 by S. S. Teulon survived, becoming a billiard room on the west garden front, facing the viewer, at the right hand end of the main block. Further to the right was a bowling alley built with local carstone, making the 150m front one of the longest of any house in the land. After a fire in 1891, two more storeys of store rooms and staff bedrooms designed by Col. R. W. Edis were built over the billiard room, and the bowling alley was converted to a library in 1901. Edis had added a single-storey ballroom projecting from the south end of the opposite (entrance) front in 1883. By 1909 Sandringham's 365 rooms made it the largest English private house but ninety-one rooms in the service quarters were demolished in 1975 to simplify management.

The gardens are contrived to achieve the atmosphere of a family retreat. Edwardian parterres have gone and gardens neglected during the 1939-45 War were re-styled in a more relaxed natural way, eschewing grand vistas and valuing privacy. To the left, the formal north garden was laid out for King George VI by G. A. Jellicoe. It ends in a bank and shrubbery to screen private apartments from the eyes of visitors approaching along the main drive.

Beyond the mansion are reminders of the support services needed by a great house: to the right are the former stables, power house, wood-carving school and fire station, now a museum, and on the left are the Persimmon greenhouses and adjoining gardens, there to achieve self-sufficiency in flowers, fruit and vegetables.

Leicester Square Farm, South Creake

The farming scene

TF 866 337

This fine set of buildings was built by Thomas William Coke, and is one of the most impressive of the seventy or so farms on his 40,000-acre (c.16,000ha) Holkham estate. It is unusual in that it was designed as a whole by the prolific country house architect, Samuel Wyatt (1737-1807). He was working at Holkham in the 1790s where he was responsible for various lodges and the orangery within the park, as well as farm buildings, most notably the great barn and these buildings at South Creake for which about £3,500 was paid between 1793 and 1801.

There are several ways in which these buildings are typical of Wyatt's work. He frequently made use of curved walls, in this case stretching from the house towards the yards. His classical style combined with semi-circular openings can be seen in the barn façade. Originally the farmstead would have been an open yard with stables and cattle sheds along the sides, and two corner pavilions containing feed stores with granaries and haylofts above. The other two corners contained matching shepherd's and bailiff's cottages. The yard was subdivided by shelter sheds in the 1870s.

Approached from the east, the barn façade, flanked by the identical pavilions at the corner of the yard, presented an architectural symmetry of which no farmer need be ashamed. The elegant farm house looked outwards across a park-like home pasture in which the tenant could have believed himself a gentleman. From the back he looked into his cattle yard where, during the winter, the basis of agricultural prosperity, the farmyard manure, would have accumulated. This planned farm shows a transitional layout from the mid eighteenth-century plan where the farm house was very much part of the yard, to the nineteenth-century type where the rising social status of the farmer meant that his house was built at a distance from his work place.

The farming scene

80 Water meadows, Castle Acre, 1946

TF 821 150

The problem of feeding animals through the spring as stored winter supplies were becoming short was one that had to be faced by farmers before the days of manufactured feeds. It was partly solved by the growing of root crops, but the encouragement of an early growth of grass by the creation of water meadows was another solution. A system of leets and sluices ensured that the meadows were flooded under a sheet of gently moving water from October until March. Because the water was moving it would not normally freeze, and so as well as providing extra moisture, kept the ground warm, providing the necessary stimulus for the grass to grow, producing an early bite up to six weeks before naturally growing pasture.

The creation of water meadows was an expensive business (contemporaries estimated something between £10 and £40 an acre) and so it was only taken up in Norfolk by a few of the wealthiest land owners and tenants. The largest Norfolk water meadows extend to 12ha below Castle Acre castle. They were laid out shortly after 1803 by Thomas Purdy, a tenant of Thomas William Coke of Holkham, and did not go out of use until just before the First World War.

Water was taken from the River Nar to the north of Newton church (towards the north-east of the picture) and fed via a brick sluice under the road to form a straight main channel running south beside the river. After about 250m this splits. Both channels then ran parallel to the river at a higher level so that water could overflow into the smaller rills and across the meadowland.

Water meadows are a common feature of the river valleys of the southern counties, but Norfolk's colder climate meant that the meadows did sometimes freeze. However, the suitability of Norfolk's soils to the growing of turnips meant that the problem of winter feed was not as great here as elsewhere. Those water meadows that do survive are a monument to the spirit of experiment which was so much part of the Agricultural Revolution in the county.

Radial pig-farming, Hoe

The farming scene

81

TF 992 174

This photograph shows a field at Hoe set out for use by a herd of outdoor pigs. The centre of the radial is the collecting point for pigs entering and leaving the individual 'paddocks' - via the vehicle roadway at the lower left 8 o'clock position. The paddocks are divided by electric fences, and have water troughs and wallows against the periphery. The pig huts are grouped together within each paddock.

The pigs in the radial system are the 'in-pig' sows; they stay in this area until a week before they are due to give birth and then they are moved to farrowing huts in the next field. Some of the individual farrowing huts can be seen at the mid left edge of the photograph.

The top left-hand corner shows round bales in the harvest field, some of which have been collected for the straw to be used as litter in the pig huts. Young pigs are reared in covered accommodation in the twelve 'sty' type movable kennels next to the bales.

The field will be cropped with cereals and sugar beet after two years with pigs, as part of a five-year rotation.

The farming scene

82 Tunstead traditional harvest scene

TG 302 221

Although taken in 1995 this view belongs to an age of farming which has long since passed. The type of reaper binder seen here at work was developed in America in the 1840s and was a commonplace sight on the harvest fields for over a hundred years. Pulled originally by horses and then by tractors, they were eventually replaced in the 1960s by the combine harvester.

The straw left over from the harvesting would have been a valuable asset around the farm and in the rural countryside. Straw was used for thatching buildings and providing bedding and litter for farm livestock. Chopped into small pieces, known as chaff, it was mixed with feed for over-wintering livestock. When added to clay it makes clay lump, one of the primary building materials of the county.

Straw that has been through a combine is useless for thatching. Thatching requires the straw to be long and unbroken. Modern cereal varieties have been selectively bred to provide more corn and less straw. A few farms still grow the old long-strawed varieties and harvest them with old-fashioned machinery like the reaper binder to provide straw for thatching.

The sheaves of straw can be seen in the photograph lying in regular rows where they have come off the binder. They are then collected and stood up in groups, called stooks, to finish ripening. The stooks show as darker rows.

Cereal farming, Themelthorpe

TG 063 241

The farming scene

83

The pattern and rhythm of the farming year has changed over the last century but most rapidly in the past thirty years. Here the tractor is already hard at work on the recently harvested cereal field. The straw bales have not even been collected from the field before the plough is brought in to begin to break up the soil and plough in the stubble. The bales will be collected as the tractor ploughs up and down the field. In some cases the field will be ploughed, rolled and drilled within the same day or within a couple of days of ploughing.

The large and powerful tractors that are now available to the modern farmer allow him to plough between fifteen and twenty acres (6 to 8ha) a day using ploughs capable of turning up to five furrows at a time. In the days of horse ploughing, the ploughman and his horse would average about three-quarters of an acre (0.3ha) a day using a single furrow plough, and walk twelve miles in the process. This did not include the distance travelled to and from the farm before and after work!

In the past the harvest would be collected, then livestock and poultry would be turned out onto the fields to feed on any ears of corn left behind by the harvesters. They would then be kept on the fields to feed on the first grass that came after harvest, or on the undersown crop, usually of clover. Their dung would provide the manure for the next crop. Once they had fed off the field, then ploughing would begin. Teams of horses and later, tractors, would plough the soil, usually twice, before the seed was drilled in for the next season.

The farming scene

84 Stubble burning at Salle

TG 101 256

The practice of stubble burning really developed as a result of the increased production of cereal crops during the 1970s. The development of the European Economic Community, now the European Union, and the payment of agricultural subsidies and guaranteed prices for cereal crops led to an enormous increase in the acreage of land given over to cereal production. The drawback to the expansion of cereal growing was that the amount of stubble left after the harvest also increased enormously.

Straw is difficult to dispose of because it takes a long time to rot down. In the old scheme of farming it was left to the action of the weather to break down the stubble. The land would then be cultivated after a reasonable period of time had elapsed. It would again be left to weather before being ploughed, then harrowed, rolled and drilled.

The new order of cereal growing did not allow time for this to happen. The remedy was to get rid of the stubble by burning it off the fields. It was argued that the resulting ash released a small amount of nutrient into the soils when ploughed in and that weed seeds and possible plant diseases were destroyed by the fires. It also allowed another cereal crop to be sown almost immediately after harvesting the previous one. This was the practice that was followed for about twenty years.

The end came in the late 1980s when a number of serious traffic accidents occurred, involving large numbers of vehicles on motorways and main roads adjacent to cereal fields where stubble burning reduced visibility to such a degree that multi-vehicle pile-ups resulted. There was also growing pressure from residents in areas affected by the ash from the fields and also from fires that got out of control. Today loose straw is either baled and removed or chopped up and scattered before ploughing.

Caley Mill Lavender Farm, Heacham

The farming scene

85

TF 684 374 Open

Caley Mill was constructed in the early nineteenth century to a 'Gothic' design by the Le Strange family who were then the landowners. The mill was built of carstone which came from a quarry at Snettisham, and it had a large iron undershot water wheel which was removed and melted down during the Second World War.

Norfolk Lavender Ltd, the only full-scale lavender farm in England, was founded in 1932 by Linn Chilvers, a local nurseryman, and Francis (Ginger) Dusgate, a landowner from Fring. In the first year they planted 2.4ha of lavender and by 1939 they had 40ha, approximately the same as today. The company acquired the site from the Le Strange family in 1936.

The main road at the bottom of the photograph was constructed in 1953, when the layby and kiosk were also built. The modern barns to the rear were erected in two phases, the first one in 1974 in order to dry lavender, and the adjoining smaller 'half barn' was added in 1979 in order to house the distillery which had, until then, been at Fring. The conservatory near the main road was erected in 1985.

Until the mid 1960s the company was primarily a lavender grower, but then it started to diversify into the production of lavender-fragranced toiletries. In the late 1970s the barn adjoining the Mill was converted into a tearoom to cater for the increasing number of visitors which now total about 150,000 annually.

Just below the car park at the top of the picture is the herb garden, the chequer-board area on the right-hand side of the roadway running east to west through the site. Adjoining that is the path which leads to the National Collection of Lavenders.

The farming scene

86 The Royal Norfolk Show, Costessey

TG 150 103 Open

In the eighteenth and early nineteenth centuries Norfolk led the way in English agricultural development with the annual Holkham Sheep Shearings. The Norfolk Agricultural Association was formed in 1847 by the amalgamation of the West Norfolk Agricultural Association (formed in 1834) and the East Norfolk Agricultural Association (formed in 1842), and in 1908 the Association became the Royal Norfolk Agricultural Association by order of Edward VII. The Show was peripatetic until 1954. In the early years sites around the county were chosen for rail access and later as motor transport developed many large estates hosted the Show.

The Costessey Showground was purchased in 1952 and since 1954 has been the permanent home of the Royal Norfolk Show. The Show is now one of the largest two-day Agricultural Shows in the country with an average attendance, based on the years 1994-1998, of 94,000 compared to 58,000 in 1958. It remains strongly agricultural, promoting the improvement of livestock, husbandry, machinery and encouragement of agricultural science and education.

Over time the site has been extended and developed to meet modern standards with the construction of toilet blocks, grandstands, members' pavilion, livestock buildings and road networks. This 1987 photograph was taken before the construction of the Norwich southern bypass. The large area of marquees in the centre is the Flower Show. Immediately to the left can be seen the Dog Show, and immediately above are the livestock rings and buildings housing more than 2,500 large livestock. At the centre top is the Grand Ring and immediately behind is the office and members' pavilion complex.

Heydon	Villages
TG 114 273 Open	87

Heydon is one of the 'prettiest' villages in Norfolk; it is an almost classic closed village - that is, it has been in the ownership of a succession of families as a compact estate since the early sixteenth century. This overall ownership has meant, in this case, that change has been limited and slow.

The photograph shows the southern edge of Heydon Park; the present Hall (built around 1581-4) is just off to the bottom of the print. The rectangular village, with the church on its northern side dominates the area.

Heydon had a market by 1310 but with others close by at Aylsham, Cawston, Reepham and Salle it must have had to struggle for survival. The market was where there is now a green to the south of the church: the Holt to Reepham road then ran north-south through the market place and Faden's map of 1797 shows the park road visible in the foreground then serving as the east to west road linking Wood Dalling to the Holt road. The present east-west road in the distance dates from the enclosure of Heydon Common and an early nineteenth-century extension of the park. The landscape of Heydon parish is a good example of the way in which an estate - in this case of the Dynne, Earle and Bulwer families - can re-organise an earlier road systems, create a parkland landscape, and rebuild a village of attractive seventeenth- and eighteenth-century brick houses facing the green.

The church of St Peter and St Paul is a beautiful building, largely late perpendicular, with an altered clerestory. The Bulwer mausoleum visible on its north side was built in 1864. The interior is well worth a visit, with surviving fourteenth-century wall paintings and an impressive range of monuments.

Villages

88 Worstead

TG 301 260 Open

This view is from the south-west of the church looking north-eastwards. The tight cluster of buildings grouped around the small market square, Church Plain, to the east of the chancel makes it a very attractive flint and brick settlement.

As the photograph shows, the church of St Mary is externally largely a perpendicular rebuild of around 1380 with a fine range of ten clerestory windows and a handsome south porch. The chancel has remnants of the decorated style. No architectural evidence remains of the church which was recorded as being in existence in 1066. Worstead, like North Walsham, was one of the many manors in this part of Norfolk that belonged to St Benet's Abbey until the Dissolution when it came into the hands of the bishops of Norwich.

Worstead and the region around it was famous for the making of worsted cloth from c.1350 to c.1700. This cloth, made from long staple wool, was thinner and of finer quality than other woollen cloths and commanded higher prices. The profits from the cloth made the population of the area wealthy enough to erect fine perpendicular churches and red brick and flint houses of quality. The houses round the Church Plain show evidence of high rooms for cloth looms. Certainly they are impressive - especially the Manor House (hidden in the trees north of the church). Continental prosperity is reflected in the 'Flemish' gable of around 1680 on a brick house facing the church. The white house to the south of that has a high quality vaulted brick undercroft which may have been a cellar for wool storage.

Worstead is now famous for its July festival when many aspects of its textile making days are revived. The building under construction in the foreground is the Village Hall which was opened by the Queen Mother in 1985.

Attleborough is a small market town at the meeting point of a north to south road from Watton to Diss and the main Norwich to London road. The photograph is looking east with the Watton road on the left hand edge, just below centre, and the Diss road leaving the right-hand edge, near the top of the picture, leading to the railway station on the Norwich to Thetford line, opened in 1845. The Norwich to London road runs diagonally from top left to bottom right.

The town has a distinctive plan, with the main Norwich to London road running through the market place (Queen's Square, centre left). A back lane, Connaught Road, runs parallel to this to the south of the church. The contrast between the older tenements lining the main road and market place and the villas of the nineteenth century along Connaught Road is striking. Many of the tenements lining the main street are sixteenth- and seventeenth-century timber-framed buildings. Connaught Road was virtually open country at the time the tithe map was drawn in 1838. At the east end of Connaught Road is the Royal Hotel on the corner leading to the station.

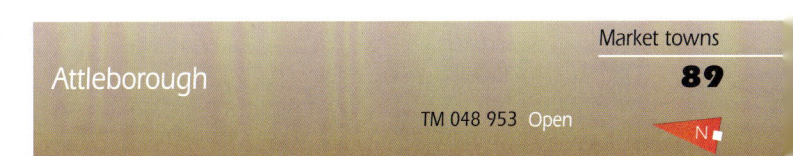

Attleborough

Market towns

TM 048 953 Open

The major building in Attleborough is the parish church of St Mary which was a large cruciform collegiate church. The unusual east tower was in fact the central tower of what must have been an impressive Norman church. The surviving nave and aisles are fourteenth-century in the decorated style as the west window clearly shows. A large timber-framed rectory lies in the wooded area south of the church. The medieval college may have been where the large store east of Queen's Square now stands. A fine timber-framed building was demolished there in the 1970s.

Market towns

90 Aylsham

TG 190 272 Open

The market town of Aylsham is dominated by the handsome church of St Michael with its decorated tower and nave with perpendicular transepts and a fine porch dating from 1488. The church, in a generous churchyard, is close to the market place on its north side and the Old Vicarage in turn bounds the churchyard.

The main south to north axis, Red Lion Street, is the Norwich to Cromer road which is crossed at the south-east corner of the Market Place by the road from Bawdeswell to North Walsham and the coast: an ancient route for pilgrims to Bromholme Priory. The Cromer road having skirted the churchyard drops sharply down to the meadows of the Bure valley. Away to the north east off the photograph, Millgate is a separate element of Aylsham which formed around the head of the Bure Navigation, built in the late eighteenth century. Two railway stations also served Aylsham from 1882 and 1883 respectively.

The attractive market place dates from at least 1296. A series of sixteenth- and seventeenth-century tenements forms its western edge, while others on its southern side have been replaced by modern development. Red Lion Street is another almost complete sixteenth- and seventeenth-century street, as is White Hart Street which branches off it to the north-east. The nineteenth-century Town Hall (1856) has replaced earlier infill into the market place and what appears to be infill between the market and Red Lion Street has several fine buildings in it; the southern courtyard block dates from the sixteenth or early seventeenth centuries. There are many other high quality brick buildings in Aylsham including a number of houses with so-called Flemish or Dutch gables.

Downham Market is situated on the edge of the Fens close to the River Ouse and at the junction of two main routes, Swaffham to Wisbech and King's Lynn to Cambridge. The Ouse provided an important trade route, especially by the seventeenth century. This view of the town clearly shows narrow tenements facing the main thoroughfares, typical of medieval and later development.

The Norman church stands at the highest point and there was a Benedictine Priory site nearby, of which very little remains. The market place (top left, below car park) lies at the junction of Bridge Street and the High Street. Downham was a major trading place for dairy produce, shipped to Cambridge via the river. By the eighteenth century it seems to have declined as its rivals grew. The large butter market was closed but the horse and livestock fairs lasted into the present century. Building development continued, including four substantial coaching inns, and an increased use of brick is evidence of ongoing wealth creation.

The nineteenth century and the coming of the railway (1846) saw much redevelopment. Older buildings were demolished to make way for the Town Hall (1887) on the far side of the market place. At the market corner stands the gothic-style cast-iron clock (1878). Four chapels, a Courthouse (1849), the Union Workhouse (1836) and several maltings were erected as the town's fortunes improved.

Recent changes include the shopping centre behind the Town Hall and the demolition of older buildings near the church, but the medieval town centre plan has remained essentially unchanged.

Market towns

Downham Market

TF 612 033 Open

91

Market towns

92 Fakenham

TF 919 296 Open

Although the chief manor belonged to the Crown and a market was granted in 1250, Fakenham was little more than a large village in the Middle Ages. The tax assessment of 1334 places it 68th in value in the county, below places like North and South Creake. In 1603 its population was only about 500, but its market survived when others dwindled and vanished, and it became an important centre for the sale, for example, of groceries and spices, while a market-day sermon set up in 1610 testifies to its drawing-power. Encroachments on the market place, spreading south from the church and north from the Tunn Street area (extreme left) during the Middle Ages, had become stabilised into permanent buildings by 1650, when a map shows the street pattern and building lines much as they are today. A 'sessions house', built by an innkeeper to boost trade, stood on the site later occupied by the Corn Hall (the large free-standing building left of the church), and a rate assessment of 1650 lists sixty-eight houses, three inns, and five shops. In 1664 there were at least seventy-eight houses, besides those inhabited by the poor. Fire destroyed twenty-six buildings on the east side of the market place (bottom centre) in 1738. By 1801 there were 1,236 people living in 237 houses; the population contining to grow.

The railway reached Fakenham in 1848, with a second line coming in 1880. In 1855 the building of the Corn Hall, containing corn exchange, magistrates' room, assembly room, reading room and library, symbolised the town's prosperity and aspirations. By 1883, when the population was nearly 2,800, there were 175 shops, businesses, manufacturers, and services. Most of the buildings in the photograph have eighteenth- or nineteenth-century facades, many, like those of the Crown and the Red Lion (bottom centre, facing each other) concealing backs or interiors of the sixteenth or seventeenth centuries. Although the population is now about 6,000, the development of out-of-town industries and supermarkets has caused the market place to suffer an economic decline.

Great Yarmouth

Market towns

93

TG 524 077 Open

The heart of Yarmouth is shown with the great parish church of St Nicholas, founded in 1101, facing south towards the big market place. The market place is the remnant of an even larger plain that until King Street was laid out in the 1670s ran the full length of the town. In the foreground is the new covered market. To the left of the photograph is Howard Street, formerly Blind Middlegate, the curving spine road of medieval Yarmouth; and running east and west from it are lines of buildings which, though the rows themselves have largely succumbed to Second World War bomb damage and subsequent redevelopment, represent the 145 'rows' or lateral passages that were a unique feature of the Yarmouth settlement pattern. Historians argue whether this pattern was the result of early medieval town planning or whether it arose naturally from quayside development pushing towards an ever westward-moving river. It is likely that the rows themselves followed boundaries separating the original burgage plots into which the town was divided by the late twelfth century. The pattern is best preserved in the section above the car park at the bottom of the photograph, though even here the marks of a recent devastating fire can be seen. The impression remains of extremely tightly-packed sixteenth-century and later housing in the row area.

In front of the parish church stands the early fourteenth-century hall of the Benedictine Priory and the market place is cut across by a modern two-lane highway. The town wall, begun in 1285, shows to the left of the car park in the top right-hand corner of the photograph. It continues south until it is obscured by the Market Gates shopping mall, which in fact straddles and preserves it. Outside the wall the pattern is of fingers of nineteenth-century development along roads leading to the sea.

Market towns

94 Holt

TG 078 387 Open

At the confluence of roads is the war memorial, the site of the original market. This, with its two annual fairs, was the source of Holt's prosperity. For a long while the town was known as Holt Market. Below the war memorial in the picture is one of the three manors of the town, now known as the Old School House, the site of the original Gresham's School, founded in 1555. To the right of this traffic island is the area known as Fish Hill, whose shops stand on the sites of the former market stalls where the great fire of Holt of 1708 started. This destroyed at least half the town, which was then rebuilt in brick in the Georgian style, epitomised by the Feathers Hotel, the old coaching inn, situated in the High Street to the left of the pedestrian crossing. To the right of this crossing is one entrance to the many lokes or alleyways to be found in Holt.

In the triangular space formed by the junction of three roads (just above centre) is the Shire Hall, a tall, white, free-standing building which was once the Magistrate's Court. Facing it across the plain to the north-east is an early seventeenth-century range with medieval cellars. This could have been a merchant's house or one of the missing manor houses. The road to the right of the central block of houses and shops is Bull Street, named after one of the many public houses that used to fill the town. The three-storey building on this street is dated 1744 on the gable and has over its door an early insurance plaque. At the extreme right is the single-storey post office near to the site of a Quaker Chapel.

Saturday Market Place, King's Lynn

Market towns

TF 617 198 Open

The market place by the Lynn (or estuarine pool or lake) was a focus for traders in salt and fish before 1101 when the Bishop of Norwich recognised the town on the western edge of his Gaywood estate. Here was founded the priory church of St Margaret complete with twin towers and cloister. Rebuilt and enlarged in later centuries and a symbol of medieval ecclesiastical lordship, it continues to dominate the town from the west, though Bishop's Lynn became King's Lynn in 1537. The hub of economic and political power had already relocated to the fifteenth-century Trinity Guildhall, standing proudly on the other side of the Saturday Market Place and still the Town Hall today. It tells of the enormous wealth generated by Lynn's merchants from home and foreign trade, much of which was invested in building, not least on the land claimed from the river, to the west of the original bank formed by Nelson and Queen Streets, to the south and north of the market place respectively. Of some significance is the rectangular complex known as St Margaret's House, just to the south-west of the church, where the greater part of the late fifteenth-century trading post of the Hanseatic League survives. None other remains in England. The South Quay was made from a sand bank in the 1850s and has served as one of Lynn's many car parks (Vol.1: 85).

Market towns

96 Tuesday Market Place, King's Lynn

TF 617 208 Open

The Norwich bishops were probably surprised by the rapid growth of their new town of Lynn, northwards from the Saturday Market Place. In the 1140s Bishop Turbe laid out a second town or 'Newland' between the Purfleet and the Gaywood river, really a planned suburb of the first, but with its own generous market place. This remains an impressive feature of the town, seen here on a Tuesday market day, overlooked by fine buildings of the seventeenth and eighteenth centuries. By 1400 sufficient land had been claimed from the river to the west of the market place to establish a new landing stage. This Common Staithe is today occupied by the Corn Exchange of the 1850s and a car park. Yet more *terra firma* was acquired to the west of King Street which was once the river bank between the Purfleet and the Tuesday Market Place; in the foreground the long plots developed down to the Ouse can be seen, above all, the Guildhall of St George (c.1430) and its warehouses. The merchants responsible for its erection were also involved in the rebuilding of the Chapel of St Nicholas, founded by Bishop Turbe to the north-east of the market place and the religious heart of Lynn's fishing community - 'the North End'. The office blocks and car parks of the 1970s visible now in this area confirm its fate.

North Walsham

Market towns

TG 282 302 Open

The church of St Nicholas stands squarely in its churchyard which has been cleared of tombstones. It was damaged during the Peasant's Revolt of 1381 but survived the fire of 1600 which destroyed 118 houses, together with barns, malthouses, shops and warehousing. The tower, which was 45m high, collapsed in 1724 and another portion fell in 1835 and has never been restored. The market place to the south of the church is still fronted by substantial shops, many once houses with business premises beneath. Narrow streets, known as 'lokes', ran south from the market place. Their parallel form suggests some attempt at town planning after the fire of 1600. To the north-west of the church a shopping precinct and car park have replaced early cottages and lanes. The right-angled bend into Market Street skirts what was the Butchery at the west end of the churchyard. The tiered canopy of the market cross is clearly seen at the west end of the market place. This cross was built by Bishop Thirlby in the reign of Edward VI, and repaired in 1600 by Bishop Redman. It remains an important feature and has formed the centre point for many celebrations in the town, from a feast to celebrate the accession of William IV, coronation feasts of later monarchs, to War Weapons Weeks in the Second World War.

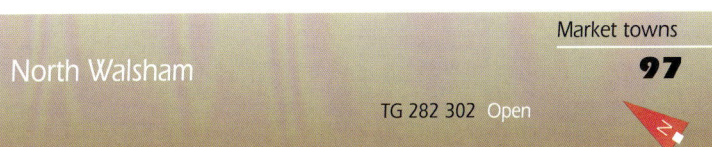

Market towns

98 Swaffham

TF 819 089 Open

Swaffham has no castle, priory nor accessible river, yet it has become an important social and market centre for central west Norfolk (Vol.1: 81). It lies on the main Norwich to King's Lynn road (A47) where it is crossed by the south to north road from Thetford to the north coast (A1065). Swaffham was granted a market here in 1215.

The triangular market place dominates this view. The large parish church of St Peter and St Paul is set back well behind the eastern tenements. The patterns of tenements around the three sides of the market place is very noticeable, with a back lane or service lane showing clearly to the west.

The northern half of the market has gradually been filled in. The butchers' shambles lay between the Town Hall and the A47. The Corn Hall, reflecting the importance of the grain trade in the local economy, was built in 1858. The Assembly Rooms, very much a social centre for the landed gentry of the eighteenth century, face the open market place. The market cross was built by the Earl of Orford in 1783. Faden's map of Norfolk, 1797, has a large-scale inset map of Swaffham which shows much less infill in the market place and a large horse pond to the south-east of the cross, but the continuous rows of buildings around the market were already in place.

The façades on the north side of the market place can be seen to be handsome and there are several very fine late seventeenth- and eighteenth-century buildings facing it on its western and eastern sides, for example, Hammonds School, built around 1736. The parish church is a largely perpendicular building, much of it late perpendicular with a clerestory of thirteen windows and transepts. The interior has a high-quality hammer-beam roof.

Watton is a small market town lying on the eastern edge of Breckland. It is on the line of a major Roman road that led from Caistor St Edmund via Crownthorpe on to Denver and the Fen Causeway. The road from Thetford to Dereham crosses this axis at Watton providing a good site for a market. Watton grew westwards, extending the main street after the parliamentary enclosure in 1803, and eastwards during the Second World War with the construction of an airfield.

Watton is a linear settlement with no obvious focal point: the market stalls can be seen lining the left hand side of the High Street. The parallel Back Street lies to the left (north) of the High Street. A cluster of small properties fills the space between these two streets and those at the point where the two roads splay out may mark a former open market area. The main road through the town crosses the north to south road at this point. The Tithe Map of 1839 shows very few properties to the left of Back Street and all the area on the left-hand side of the photograph is recent housing infill. The Norman church of St Mary lies outside the town off the top edge of the picture.

Watton's market existed by 1204 and in the seventeenth and eighteenth centuries it was famous as a butter market.

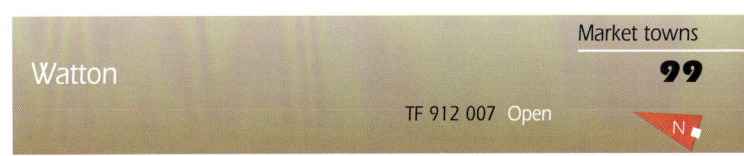

Market towns
Watton
99
TF 912 007 Open

The Wissey valley downstream of Watton opens out westwards as an eastern arm of the Fens and the grazing marshes of these fens supported large numbers of cattle. The brecks supported sheep. A fire swept Watton in 1674 and unlike Wymondham, Watton was rebuilt in brick and flint rather than in timber. There are few dominant buildings in Watton to compare with Swaffham. Watton's railway, the Thetford to Swaffham line, arrived in 1875 and closed in 1964.

Market towns

100 Wymondham

■N   TG 109 015 Open

This view is taken looking west over the core of the town to the abbey (Vol.1: 35) and its precincts and across the shallow valley of the River Tiffey. A short stretch of the Wymondham to Dereham railway is just visible running through the river meadows. This line was opened in 1847 and closed in 1970; it is now being repaired to allow its re-opening.

The remains of Wymondham's Benedictine abbey dominate the western third of the photograph. The abbey was founded by William d'Albini in 1107 and was dissolved in 1534. The site of the choir lies in the triangle to the east of the central tower and the east gable of the chapter house still stands. The nave, west tower and the rebuilt aisles survive as the present parish church. Fortunately much of the precinct to the south of the abbey, with widespread earthworks, survives to give a perfect setting for the ruins.

Under the protection of both William d'Albini (butler to King Henry I) and the priory, a market town developed outside the east gate of the precinct, but a fierce fire in 1615 burnt much of the town. Many of its buildings, such as the market cross in the centre of the market, were rebuilt, still using timber in many cases. Timber-framed buildings line the streets which radiate from the market place and also Damgate which skirts the east wall of the Abbey precinct. The east window of Becket's Chapel, now the library, can be seen just to the west of the point where the Market Place funnels towards the east gate of the Abbey.

Norwich 1917 photomosaic

TG 231 085 Open

This fine air photomosaic - the oldest surviving photograph of its type in Britain - is composed of dozens of vertical photographs taken in May 1917. Carefully scaled, matched, spliced and joined together to form this single image, it is a testament to the skill of the photographers of 9 Training Squadron, Royal Flying Corps, which was based at Mousehold Aerodrome. The aerodrome was established in October 1914 on some 106ha of Mousehold Heath, traditionally used as a cavalry training ground. The 75ha remnant of the Heath, between Britannia Barracks and Mousehold Lane, here seen criss-crossed with footpaths, was given to the city by the dean and chapter of the cathedral in 1885.

Norwich, the largest medieval city in England, dominated by the Norman castle and the cathedral, is set within an oxbow of the River Wensum and defended to the south-west by the city wall. The importance of Norwich as a centre of trade can be seen from the number of roads which radiate from the twelve gates which pierced the medieval defences.

The impact of the railways is evidenced by the three stations which respect the walls of the medieval city. City Station, off Barn Road, was built in 1882 by the Midland and Great Northern and closed in 1959; Victoria Station, built in 1849 on the site of Victoria Gardens and converted to freight traffic in 1916, was closed in 1966; Norwich Thorpe, built in 1844, and rebuilt by the Great Eastern Railway in 1886, is now the city's only rail terminus. Contemporary with the period of railway expansion are the great areas of terraced, urban housing to the south-west of the walled city, built between 1849 and 1884 on land formerly owned by Colonel C. W. Unthank (originally known as the 'New City') (Vol.1: 99). A similar development to the north was built on land reclaimed from Mousehold Heath between 1880 and 1908 (Vol.1: 98).

Norwich

102 Norwich market place, 1921

TG 229 085 Open

This photograph, taken by the late George Swain, depicts Norwich market place in 1921. Laid out in an area known as Mancroft, after either *magna crofta* (great fields) or *maene croft* (common field), between 1066 and 1075, the market stood on open land to the west of the Great Cockey, a tributary of the River Wensum.

Leading from the Haymarket, past St Peter Mancroft Church towards the Guildhall, is St Peter's Street (or Market Street). Stalls cluster between Gentleman's Walk and the Municipal Buildings. Buildings to the east of the church probably represent the sites of earlier market stalls suggesting that they encroached upon a formerly wider street.

The Guildhall, the largest outside London, stands on the site of the Market Tollhouse and south of the site of the Worsted Seld, where the quality of cloth, the most important trade commodity in the medieval city, was assessed.

To the west, in a building on one of the tenement plots facing onto St Peter's Street, James Smith opened a ready-made shoe-shop in 1792. Developed by his grandson, Charles Winter, to occupy the whole frontage between Wounded Hart Lane and Graham's Court, the family business became 'Start-rite Shoes', celebrating its bicentenary in 1992 with an unbroken tradition of employing between 800 and 900 local people to produce quality footware. Between the Start-Rite factory and St Giles stood a splendid Georgian Mansion, 'Low Court', the home of H. Frederick Low, the accomplished aerial photographer of the Norfolk and Norwich Aero Club, from 1932 to 1939. Low Court, and all the buildings to the west of the Market Place, were demolished in 1936 in order to make way for the new City Hall, which now overlooks the enlarged market place.

Norwich market place and City Hall, c.1938

TG 229 085 Open

These three next photographs show the area of the market place and City Hall over a period of some sixty years. The first view (103) was taken by H. Frederick Low of the Norfolk and Norwich Aero Club in about 1938 and shows construction of City Hall well-advanced with the central and southern wings complete and work progressing on the clock tower. The building had been the subject of a design competition which was eventually won by the architects C. H. James and S. Rowland Pierce. Work began in 1936 and proceeded rapidly, the building being ready for its official opening in October 1938 by King George VI and Queen Elizabeth. The lions (by Alfred Hardiman) at the front of the building are already on their plinths in this photograph; one of these had been exhibited at the British Empire Exhibition in Glasgow in 1936 where it was seen by the architects who commissioned a second to form the pair.

The construction of City Hall was carried out in tandem with demolition of municipal buildings on the market place and the laying out of the market anew to designs by Robert Atkinson. Originally, Atkinson's designs included the demolition of the Sir Garnet Wolseley public house (north of St Peter Mancroft churchyard) but this was reprieved. The works meant that the market stalls were temporarily displaced to the area of what was to become the car park of City Hall. Immediately west of this is the slightly earlier Fire Station (top centre) built in 1932-4 to designs by Stanley Livock.

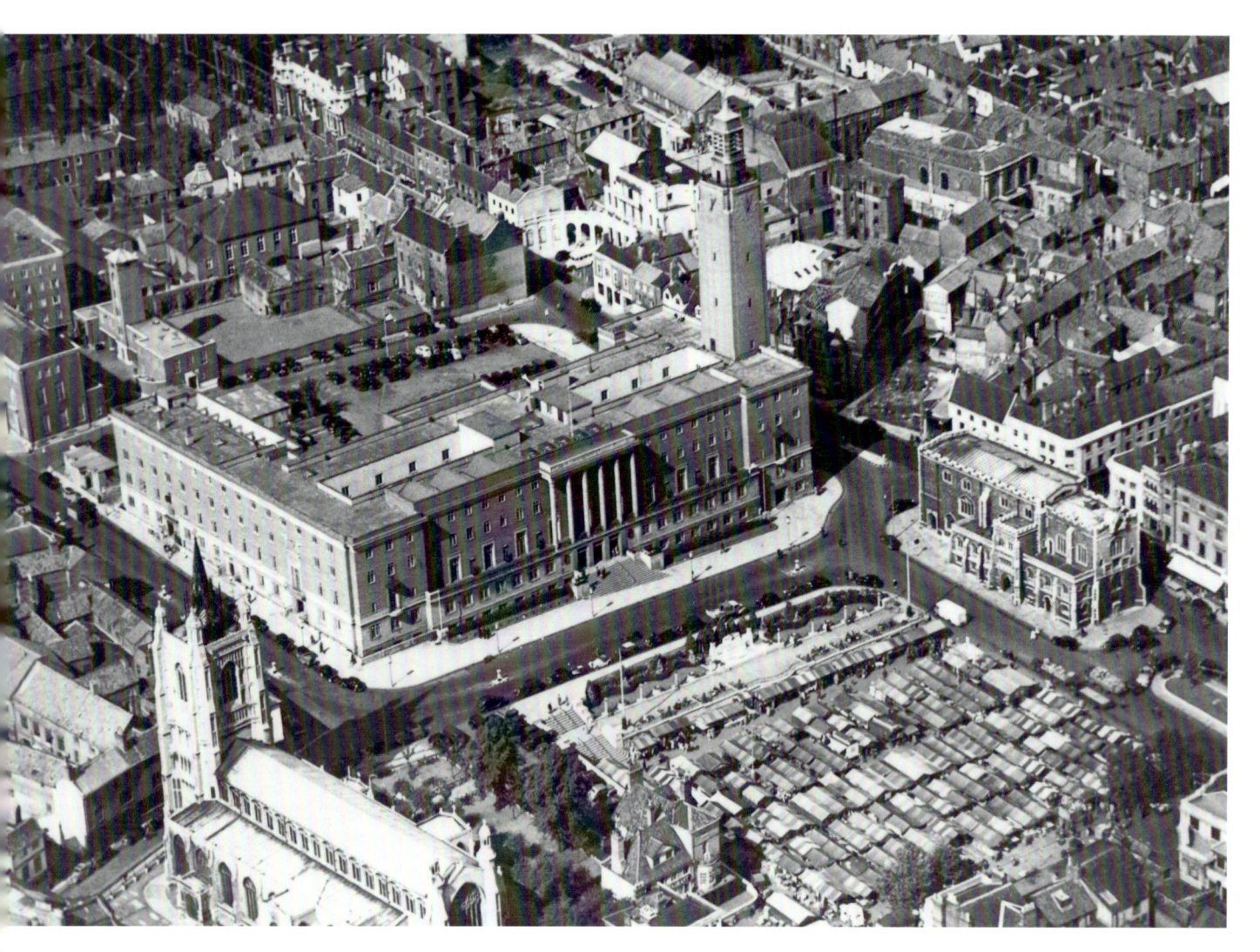

104 Norwich market place and City Hall, c.1951

TG 229 085 Open

This photograph, taken by George Swain, shows the same area in about 1951. City Hall is complete although the projected north wing, enclosing the car park from St Giles Street to the north, was never built. Between City Hall and the market place are the Memorial Gardens, laid out as part of the late 1930s scheme and incorporating Sir Edwin Lutyens' Great War memorial, which still stood at the east end of the Guildhall in the previous photograph (103), but had not been built in 1921 (102). North of City Hall is a bomb site where the Clover Leaf Cafe was destroyed in the 'Baedeker' Raids of April 1942 and the Raven public house badly damaged (subsequently demolished and rebuilt).

Westward along St Giles Street can be seen the curving colonnaded entrance to the Hippodrome. This was built as the Grand Opera House but was sold in 1904 for use as a variety theatre. Re-named the Hippodrome, it staged twice-daily shows. It suffered from a very near miss in the Baedeker Raids, one wall collapsing and the stage being lifted into the air. The building was repaired but eventually closed in 1960 and was demolished to make way for a multi-storey car park.

South of City Hall and west of St Peter Mancroft is a cluster of buildings which formed the New Star Inn. This coaching inn, dating from the fourteenth century and with a frontage on St Peter's Street, had paneled interiors and brick-vaulted undercrofts. It was demolished in 1962 in favour of the Library car park and the Central Library. The latter was designed by the then City Architect, David Percival, and received the Gold Medal of the Royal Institute of British Architects. It incorporated the Second Air Division Memorial Library in commemoration of American airmen based in Norfolk and killed during the Second World War.

Norwich market place and City Hall

TG 228 084 Open

This photograph was taken on 5th August 1994, four days after the devastating fire which destroyed the Central Library. The burnt-out shell stands top left with the blackened book stack rising above it. Originally designed around a courtyard, the building was extended in 1992 by space-frame infilling (visible as five parallel narrow roofs). The entire structure has since been demolished and is being replaced by a new Millennium Library designed by Sir Michael Hopkins and Partners.

Beyond Central Library, at the top of the photograph, can be seen the Bethel Hospital. The earliest parts date from 1712-13 and formed the first purpose-built mental hospital in the country. The complex was extended in the late nineteenth century by the local architect Edward Boardman. The hospital closed recently and currently awaits an alternative use.

East of the Library car park is the C&A building of 1968-70. It stands on Hay Hill which was redesigned with steps in 1990. A statue to Sir Thomas Browne, the seventeenth-century philosopher and physician, sits on the steps; the statue was designed by Henry Pegram in 1905 and previously stood further down the hill in the centre of a grassed area (102). The Mancroft Octagon in the south-east corner of the churchyard was built in 1983. It occupies part of the processional way which ran under the east end of the church and is used as a meeting room and cafe (Vol.1: 95).

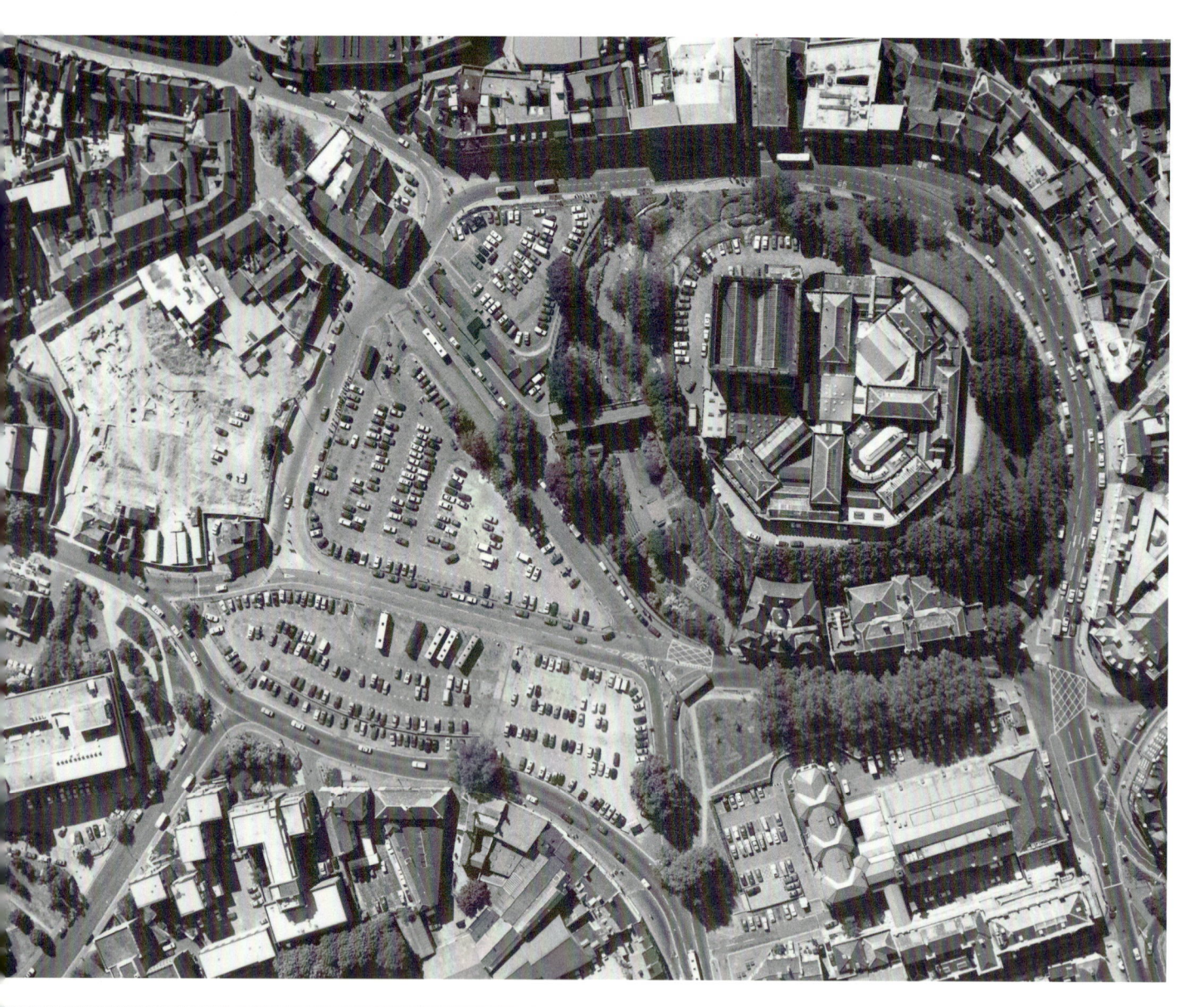

106 Norwich - Cattle Market car park and Castle Mall
Norwich

TG 231 083 Open

These next three photographs depict Norwich Castle and, in particular, the site of the Castle Mall shopping centre. The first (106) was taken on 15 June 1989 and shows the start of archaeological excavation over what was to be a 2ha site. Detailed work had at that stage only taken place on the Timberhill street frontage where the remains of medieval pits and other features can be seen.

The photograph depicts most of the extensive area of Norwich Castle which by about 1100 covered some 5.5ha. It consisted of a motte or mound upon which was constructed a great square Keep which still survives and can be seen with its twin (nineteenth-century) roofs. Beside the motte were two baileys or enclosures. The larger of these lay to the south in the area covered by the three car parks in the photograph plus a small part of the block under excavation (where cars are parked). The smaller, north-eastern, bailey lay under the site of Anglia Television (bottom, centre right), the Royal Hotel (bottom right) and Barclays Bank (centre right).

The curving line of Castle Meadow around the western and northern parts of the mound marks the line of the mound ditch. This ditch survives as the Castle Gardens to the south (where it is crossed by an early twelfth-century bridge) but has been built upon to the east. The Shirehall stands here, the larger, northern, part of which was built by William Wilkins in 1822; the smaller, roughly square, extension to the south is the work of George Skipper in 1907.

Beyond the curve of Castle Meadow can be seen a further curving street, that of London Street, Castle Street and Back of the Inns. This marks the edge of the Castle Fee or Liberty, that part of the castle outside the defences but still under royal, rather than borough, control. Land here and in the baileys passed to the city in 1345.

Norwich - Cattle Market car park and Castle Mall **Norwich 107**
TG 231 083 Open

The second photograph (107) was taken on 18 May 1992, exactly a year after the conclusion of archaeological excavation. It shows construction of the Castle Mall shopping precinct to be well-advanced but emphasises the logistical difficulties facing the designers and builders.

Castle Mall occupies the top of a ridge, the Ber Street escarpment, which falls away to the Wensum valley to the east and north (bottom and right) and to the smaller valley of the Great Cockey to the west (top). In order to provide ground floor access at various levels, exploiting the slopes of the ridge, the Mall was constructed within a very large hole, 2ha in extent and up to 20m deep. The sides of this excavation were supported by a wall of contiguous piles which extended around the perimeter of the entire construction site visible in the photograph. By the time that the photograph was taken, most of the excavation had been filled with the various levels of Castle Mall although part of the Timberhill block (left centre) remains exposed.

Roads had to be diverted and then replaced, running on 'bridges' with the new shopping precinct beneath. Such 'bridges' can be seen for Castle Meadow (between the main building site and the smaller area within a group of buildings - top centre) and Farmers' Avenue (dividing the two parts of the main construction area). In addition, a temporary bailey bridge was constructed to link the top of the castle mound with the rest of the city while work proceeded at the foot of the twelfth-century bridge. Close to the bailey bridge can be seen the long oval shape of the main shopping precinct, subsequently roofed in 'winter garden' style.

Norwich

108 Norwich - Cattle Market car park and Castle Mall

TG 231 083 Open

The third photograph (108) was taken on 27 July 1994 and shows the completed Castle Mall centre. The bailey bridge to the castle mound has been removed and the 'winter garden' roof is in place above the shopping precinct. The area has been landscaped as an urban park with five storeys of shopping and car parking beneath. The approach to the castle mound is now a serpentine road which connects the southern end of Farmers' Avenue (centre left) with the bridge; curving white lines off this road are low walls embanking the landscaping.

There are two multi-storey car parks. The larger, underground, one is approached from the east (bottom centre) where access passes beneath a recovered part of the cast-iron Duke's Palace river bridge of 1822. The smaller, above ground, car park is accessed from Farmers' Avenue and has roof parking as can be seen (left). At the time of writing, work is in progress which will replace this parking with a multiplex cinema. To the right of this a glazed atrium allows daylight into that part of the shopping mall west of Farmers' Avenue.

Norwich Sport Village

Norwich

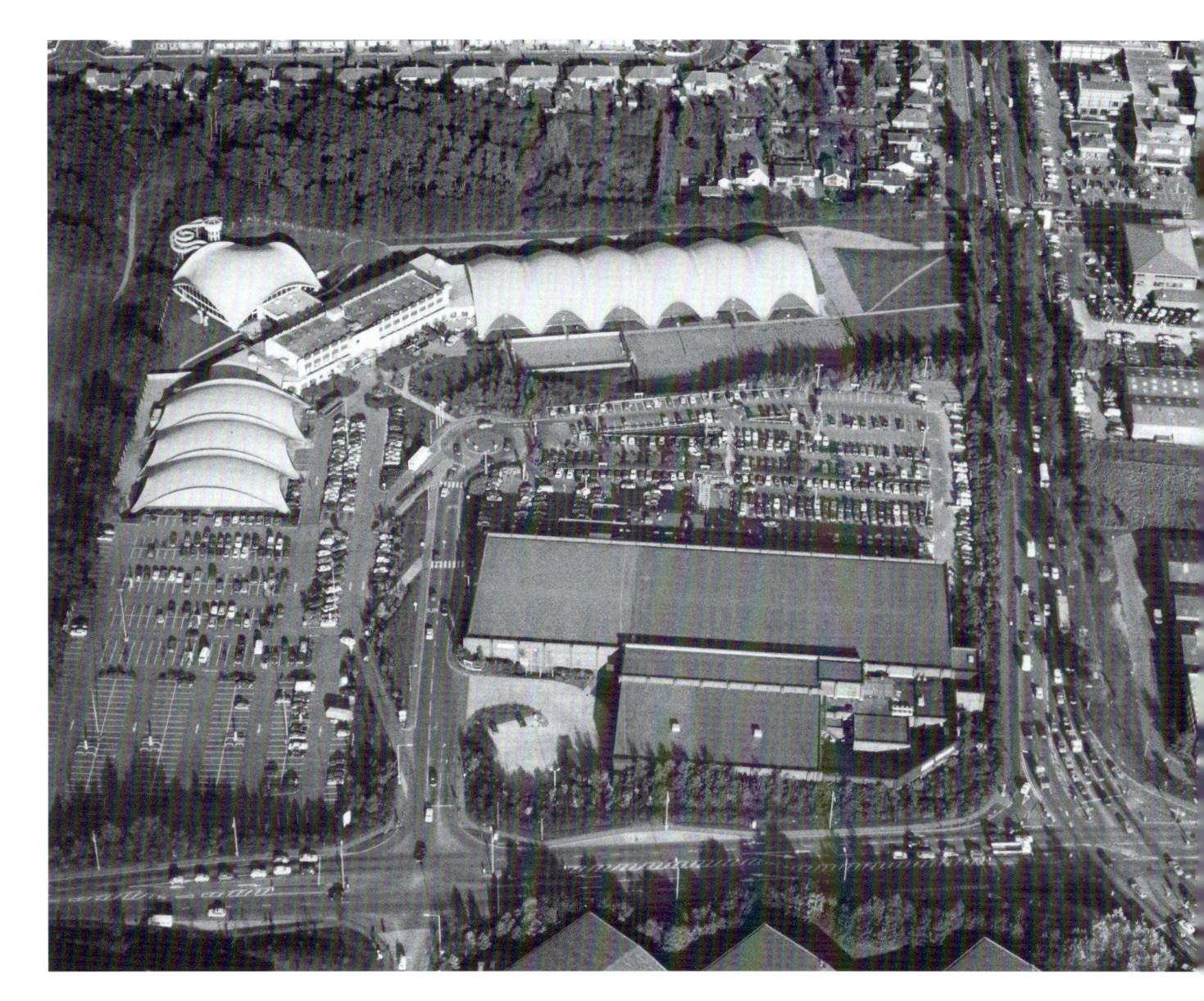

109

TG 208 112 Open

The Norwich Sport Village Hotel was opened in 1988 by the Princess Royal as a joint venture between Haus and Hero and Broadland District Council. It is a 'pay and play' sport and leisure centre, based on the Swiss concept of the family spending the day together enjoying various activities. On the left in the picture is the Wherry Hall with badminton, five-a-side, netball and basketball; on the right is the Bure with seven indoor tennis courts. The third dome, the Aquapark, was opened in 1990; it has a 25m pool, rapids, bubble bay, chutes and toddlers' pool. Sandwiched in the middle are the hotel, restaurants, bars, conference suites and, on the lower level, a Fitness Works Health Club, toning tables, beauty salon, sauna, steam and relaxation pool.

The complex is a lively and exciting place: 250,000 people come through the doors each year - all ages, shapes, sizes and abilities. The day starts at 6.30am with the Early Bird Swimmers, followed by mothers and babies, schoolchildren playing football, badminton or swimming, then old age pensioners, retired folk, tennis and badminton mornings. The locals meet regularly to enjoy exercise and leisure together. Then at 6pm there is an influx of users on their way home and the Village hums with those trying to rid the stress of the day and relax. Sunday is family day.

Occasionally, for added excitement, there are national sports events such as boxing, snooker, badminton and corporate activities including prestigious trade shows, exhibitions, meetings and charity events.

The domes, designed by Copeland Associates, are here to stay, but there are always changes. Some sports increase in popularity, while others decline; the public requires new and better facilities and investment. Chasley Hotels are the current owners and the building of a third sports hall will commence in the near future.

Norwich

110 University of East Anglia, Norwich

TG 193 075 Open

This view from the south-east shows clearly how architect Denys Lasdun's ten 'ziggurat' student residences and the massive cranked 'teaching wall', housing the teaching accommodation, (all designed and built between 1962 and 1970) exploit and enjoy this gently sloping site on the edge of Norwich city.

From the road access and main car park - top centre in the photograph - down to the artificial lake in the foreground, a raised walkway steps down the slope running parallel to the teaching wall, to which it gives access, bridging the service roads. As the ground falls away more rapidly it connects to the upper floors of six of the ziggurats and ends in a glassy bridge passing diagonally through the high-tech skin of Norman Foster's magnificent Sainsbury Centre for the Visual Arts (mid 1970s, left foreground).

This walkway also has raised links to the Library (the powerful cube behind the group of four ziggurats to the right) and to the social buildings and lecture threatres behind it. Largely hidden by these is the 'University Square' by Feilden and Mawson, its stepped open space creating a lively central focus for the community.

The dramatic, uncompromising forms of the early concrete buildings give UEA a real sense of purpose, clarity and cohesion - a sort of 'machine to study in'. Later buildings, by Rick Mather, including the serpentine residences and the courtyards of inspired informality to the right of them, benefit from rendered and ceramic finishes. As with the rest of the campus, grassy slopes and landscaping run between them, and down towards the water.

UEA is probably the most gutsy of the post-war new universities, set in a sweeping landscape and enhanced by several monumental Henry Moore sculptures. It is a splendid achievement.

Carrow Road football stadium, Norwich

TG 240 078 Open

Norwich City Football Club was formed in 1902 and played at two different grounds before its move to the current Carrow Road site in 1935. This was already in use as a sports ground for the neighbouring Boulton and Pauls' Engineering Works (now demolished, to the left). Once the decision to relocate Norwich City to Carrow Road was taken, in a remarkably short period of time, just eighty-four days, the stadium was built and nearly 30,000 fans crammed into the ground for its first ever match on 31 August 1935.

Inevitably the ground has changed much since 1935, mostly in the last twenty years or so, with only the South Stand (alongside the right-hand side of the pitch) remaining from the initial construction, although the roof and the seats within it are later additions.

Behind each goal is a 'goalpost design' two-tier stand holding approximately 6,500 people. The one at the top of the picture, built in 1992, is called the Barclay Stand (named after former Club President Evelyn Barclay) and the one at the bottom, built in 1979, is the recently re-titled Norwich and Peterborough Stand (named after former Club sponsors) - although it is familiarly known as the River End Stand, as the River Wensum runs some 45m behind it. The stand alongside the road in the photograph is the Geoffrey Watling City Stand (named after current Club President) which was built in 1986 following a fire in the old wooden Main Stand which gutted the structure in October 1984.

The current ground is an all-seater stadium with a capacity of 21,994, and although plans have been drawn to build a new South Stand, this is unlikely to happen in the near future because of financial considerations.

Industry

112 Wymondham brush factory

TG 106 022

The Co-operative Wholesale Society took over this site in 1922 and gradually transferred the whole of their brush production to Wymondham. The works closed in 1983 and the site has since been redeveloped as a housing estate. The extensive range of buildings seen here includes the drying shed for timber with the sawmill projecting from it (top centre). The ground around this shed was used to stack coppiced wood to season for use as brush stocks, mainly local birch, alder, sycamore and beech. Later drying sheds are to the right. The chimney, about 52m high, served the adjacent boiler house, where steam was generated by burning waste wood. Water was obtained from a well on the site and pumped up to the water tower, to the left of the chimney. The buildings to the left of the water tower were mainly used for wood turning for handles whilst the brushes were finished in buildings in the centre foreground. The house beside the road, bottom right, was the office block.

Lenwade concrete works, Weston Longville

Industry

TG 117 176 Open

The works started here during the Second World War, making small concrete posts, but developed rapidly after the war and became a major maker of pre- and post-stressed concrete beams for motorway bridges, employing up to 800 people. This photograph shows the works at their zenith. The storage yard spanned by two massive travelling cranes stretches nearly 550m from the bottom left of the photograph and shows the output of the works. The buildings at the top right were built to make pre-fabricated concrete sections for the construction of tower blocks of flats in London. Special trains took these to London on the rail line on the right of the photograph until a gas explosion caused the collapse of one of the blocks in 1968. Production of these sections ceased shortly after.

The main casting shops are in the middle of the photograph with long beds for stressing wires, around which concrete was poured to make the beams. Hydraulic rams were used to stress the wires. The rough ground to the right of the photograph shows old gravel pits from which gravel was originally dug for concrete.

Although the works finally closed down in 1992, the site is still virtually intact with other industries using the buildings and plant.

Industry

114 Great Yarmouth power station

TG 530 050

This power station was opened in 1958 on the South Denes in Great Yarmouth with a generating capacity of 240 mega watts and it replaced the first power station which had served the town since 1894. Originally intended to be coal-fired, it actually became oil-fired, and the vast coal yard to the south, not shown in the photograph, was not used. Oil was brought in by ship to a quay nearby in the harbour. The station became obsolete and was finally demolished in 1997. A new gas-fired generating station is to be built on the site.

The station is typical of a number built in the 1950s, being a steel frame clad with bricks, resulting in an aesthetically pleasing industrial building. The chimney, over 122m high, was a landmark for miles around Great Yarmouth. In the top right corner of the photograph are one or two of the remaining buildings of the Great Yarmouth First World War Naval Air Station, which operated flying boats from here.

Reed cutting on Hickling Broad

TG 415 209

Hickling Broad nature reserve is owned by Norfolk Wildlife Trust. Its extensive reedbeds surround the largest of the Norfolk Broads. The area is a site of international importance for wildlife such as the marsh harrier, the bittern and Britain's largest butterfly, the swallowtail.

The Broad itself is man-made, having been dug for peat and clay in the Middle Ages. The reedbeds that invaded the worked-out peat diggings and now surround the broad have a long history of human exploitation. In fact, the reedbeds comprise two very different types of vegetation that have an important economic value. The first type is the famous Norfolk reed which is used to thatch buildings. The second is saw sedge, aptly named because of the serrated edges to the leaves, which is used as the ridge capping on a thatched roof.

The management of reed and sedge beds at Hickling has traditionally been carried out by the Trust's staff and local reed cutters. After cutting using small mechanised mowers, the reed and sedge is loosely bundled before being carted to the waiting boat. The photograph was taken in the summer and so the area being cut comprises saw sedge, as reed is only cut in the winter. The sedge has been cut and over part of the area loose bundles can be seen prior to carting. By carrying out this management the reedbeds were kept clear of invading trees, such as willow, and the characteristic wildlife has survived. Unfortunately, the tradition of reed and sedge cutting has been in decline elsewhere in the Broads, for economic and social reasons, and smaller and smaller areas are being cut. This has allowed trees to invade the open landscape with an adverse impact on the wildlife and reed cutters.

The Broads
116 Filby and Ormesby Broads

TG 462 135 Open

Ormesby, Filby and Rollesby are collectively known as the Trinity Broads. Filby and Ormesby Little Broad are shown here, separated by a causeway carrying the Burgh St Margaret to Filby main road. Perhaps the most striking thing about this photograph is the proximity of the sea, looking towards Hemsby, Scratby and Norfolk's very own California. Seen from the land or water, it is easy to forget that the holiday atmosphere of Great Yarmouth is only a few miles away. The Trinity Broads are not connected to the Broads navigation. There are very few boats to be seen and no motor cruisers - only a few small day boats. It is thought that the Trinity Broads used to be connected to the navigation by the alarmingly named Muck Fleet. This still exists, leading off from Filby Broad on the right of the picture, but it is overgrown and unnavigable. What remains of the Muck Fleet joins the River Bure between Stokesby and Acle Bridge.

The main Ormesby Broad has some of the best quality water in the Broads and is in fact used for water abstraction by Essex and Suffolk Water. This is partly due to its isolated state - it has not suffered the incursions of phosphates from sewage treatment works which affected most of the Broads waters, particularly in the middle years of the twentieth century. More recently, during the 1990s, Ormesby Broad has been the site of a major 'bio-manipulation' project by the Broads Authority, to encourage even better water quality and thus to improve conditions for wildlife. Microscopic algae cause poor water quality when present in large numbers, stopping other plants and animals from flourishing. Water fleas feed on algae and can literally 'eat a broad clean' if given the right conditions to thrive. For this, fish need to be temporarily removed, as they prey on the water fleas. This bio-manipulation work at Ormesby has been very successful and it is encouraging to see how quickly improvements can happen given optimum conditions.

Acle Bridge

The Broads

TG 414 116 Open

Acle lies at the heart of the Broads, on the edge of the Halvergate grazing marshes, with the traditional open landscape of marshes, drainage dykes, drainage mills, and cattle. This is all a world away from Acle Bridge and the A1064 which joins with the A47 at Acle, one of the busiest roads in the Broads, and one which cuts right across the county from Great Yarmouth to King's Lynn.

The bridge is somewhat isolated from the main town and Acle Bridge operates almost as a hamlet, with its farm, pub, boatyard, shop and a more recent addition, a cycle hire point, indicating the changing needs of the area. It is also on the route of the Weavers' Way, the Norfolk long distance footpath which winds through the Broads and which is named after the once important Norfolk weaving industry, introduced by Flemish weavers around the twelfth century.

This new bridge was opened in November 1997, although a bridge was first recorded here in 1101. Like many well-known Broads sites, Acle Bridge is not without its ghost story, of murder and revenge, which has no doubt entertained or terrified generations of Broads holiday-makers moored up along the riverbanks. The bridge was once a favourite place for executions and criminals were hung over the side!

Adjacent to the pub is a round building with a conical, thatched roof - an example of eccentric Broads architecture. It is of uncertain origin, but is now used as a restaurant.

The Broads

118 Upton Broad

TG 388 133

Upton Broad is part of a large area of undrained fenland in the Bure valley that is still largely unpolluted, unlike other broads, because it is not directly connected to the river which lies over 1.5km away. It is therefore of immense ecological value giving us an indication of what the Broads may have looked like just a few decades ago. The fens surrounding the broad are now largely covered in trees and scrubland but up until the Second World War and even later they would have been largely treeless. The open fen would have been intensively managed, and over hundreds of years local people would have taken peat for fuel from the broad and surrounding areas.

Nineteenth-century maps indicate that the broad itself has become smaller as a result of vegetation encroachment. In 1820 the area of open water was about 12ha, but today it is only half that. The shallower water can be clearly seen, picked out by the exposed water plants that have become bleached in the summer sun. The average depth of the broad is about 1.5m. The ground covering the old broad and the peat diggings is very unstable and bounces as you walk across.

The encroachment of scrub and trees onto open fens has resulted in the dramatic decline in fenland wildlife which would have been dependent on the fen remaining free of tree cover. A priority for conserving sites such as Upton is to remove some of the trees and reinstate the traditional practices of grazing and mowing. A small area of open fen maintained by the Norfolk Wildlife Trust can be seen at the top of the picture.

Barton Turf settlement lagoons

TG 356 221

This photograph captures a moment in time at Barton, showing mud-filled 'settlement lagoons' with a winter dusting of snow. These are the result of the Broads Authority's Clear Water 2000 dredging project on Barton Broad, organised in partnership with the Millennium Commission (who have given a grant of £1.15m), the Soap and Detergent Industry Association's Environmental Trust, Anglian Water, the Environment Agency and the owners of the broad, the Norfolk Wildlife Trust. The project involves dredging, 'bio-manipulation' measures to improve water quality in parts of the broad, and also a range of small-scale projects to improve facilities for the public in the area of Barton. These include small boat and cycle hire, a short walkway to view parts of the broad, an information centre, an ecology centre to improve teaching facilities at the How Hill Environmental Centre just downstream from Barton on the River Ant, and a regular trip by electric boat from How Hill to Barton.

The lagoons are filled with liquid mud pumped from the broad which dries out so that the land can later be returned to arable farming. The mud causes no problems to the soil and at present the first filled areas are being reinstated as a field with a 'bird-seed' crop of wheat and oil-seed rape. Much of the land in the photograph already looks like an ordinary field again.

Barton itself retains the atmosphere of a traditional broads village, with its hall, church, shop, farms, cottages and staithe (to the east of the picture) where trading wherries moored up to take cargo on and off. This photograph also shows the farming landscape around the Broads, which is still an important source of employment and very much part of the local way of life.

The Broads

120 Horning boatyards

TG 346 165 Open

This picture provides an unexpected view of the Broads village of Horning. The full extent of the boatyards seen here is hidden from the traveller on the river, as well as from the visitor travelling by road. Both would be almost completely unaware of this other world hidden behind the scenes, where there are more boats than cars and more dykes or channels than lanes. A variety of cruisers, both motor and sail, as well as day boats, is very much in evidence.

Tourism plays a vital role in the economy of the Broads, providing employment and supporting the network of services - boatyards, shops, pubs, cafes, garages and other businesses, which would find it difficult to survive without the income from visitors. Holiday boats also help to ensure that the boatyard services continue to function, providing diesel, toilet pump-out, water and repairs, which are all part of the traditional Broads scene and part of the 'industrial' landscape of the Broads.

The Ferry Inn on the bend of the river has ministered to the changing demands of the public over many years, and recently the ferry here has been reinstated, run by a local boatyard. This is a small passenger ferry, one of many which were once in the Broads, but which now survive mainly as pub names. This one, however, takes passengers over to the starting point for the short walk to Cockshoot Broad, just south of the picture. Cockshoot was the site of the Broads Authority's first suction-dredging experiment carried out in the 1980s to improve water quality and benefit wildlife.

The little mill (top left, converted in the 1930s) is a good example of eccentricity in Broads building, which, while perhaps not conforming to contemporary planning practice, nevertheless provides an intriguing blend of old and new.

Wroxham Broad

The Broads

TG 310 166 Open

Wroxham is the capital of the Broads. But where is it? The town of Wroxham and the adjacent Hoveton (Vol.1: 111), divided by the River Bure, are away to the north-west of the photograph and the Broad itself appears relatively isolated and enclosed by dense 'carr' or wet woodland, where trees such as alder, buckthorn and willow flourish. They and the wet fen areas help to preserve the illusion out on the water that one is miles from anywhere, in what seems literally a different world, the world of the waterborne traveller. Wroxham is one of the largest of the broads, and sailing boats are much in evidence here, with the Norfolk Broads Yacht Club the focal point. The channel of the River Bure can be seen on the right and beyond that is Hudson's Bay, the whole area amply illustrating the labyrinthine ways of the waterways of the Broads.

The Broads developed as a holiday area at the end of the nineteenth century and has continued to attract visitors and local people - approximately 5.4 million 'visitor days' are spent annually in the Broads and about 13,000 boats (both private and hire boats) are registered there. The landscape, wildlife and wide open spaces are still the main attractions; this was underlined by the designation of the Broads in 1989 as an area with status equivalent to a national park. Holidays on the Broads still offer freedom and a sense of adventure in a safe environment - just what attracted the Victorians and Edwardians.

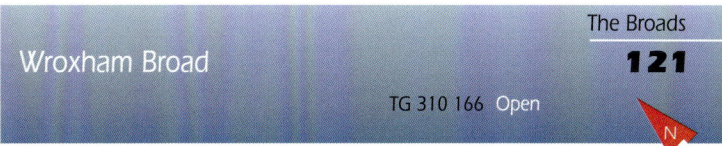

The Broads

122 Reedham car ferry

TG 407 014 Open

The last of the Broadland ferries, seen here making its crossing of the Yare at Reedham, provides a link on the B1140 from Acle to Gillingham, via the quaintly named Nogdam End. Until they fell into decay and disuse earlier this century, there were similar ferries at Buckenham and Surlingham on the Yare and at Horning and Stokesby on the Bure. Little has been recorded about the antiquity of these ferries, though it is known that Horning Ferry was called Grabbarde's Ferry in 1246; it is likely that the pontoon ferries, hauled across the river by a hand-cranked winch working on a pair of chains stretching from bank to bank, were a nineteenth-century introduction. The vehicle-carrying pontoons were known as horse ferries to differentiate them from the smaller pedestrian ferries which operated at Norwich, Whitlingham, Coldham Hall, Yarmouth and elsewhere.

The present Reedham pontoon ferry, hydraulically operated and powered by a diesel engine, was built of steel in 1983 to replace a wooden-hulled ferry which dated from 1914 and had been hand-operated until the fitting of a small motor in 1950 to power the winch that hauled the pontoon along its two chains. Proposals for a bridge at Reedham made in the 1930s and again after the Second World War were not put into effect, and although in 1934 the ferry was described by a newspaper correspondent as 'a pitiful and derelict relic of a bygone age,' it has survived as a very useful link in the local road network. The toll in 1864 was 2s.6d. (12.5p.) for a horse and carriage, and 100 years later a motor car was charged 3s.3d. (16p); today a car costs £2.

Hidden from the view of all but the aerial observer is perhaps the most enigmatic of all landscape features in Norfolk. The water gardens at Long Gore Marsh, are designed in the form of the crowned, double-headed eagle of the Greek Orthodox Church, bearing both the Papal and Patriarchal crosses and surmounting the initials 'MP' in letters of the Greek alphabet. This is the last resting place of Marietta Pallis (1882-1963) ecologist, botanist and author, and her companion Phyllis Riddle of Hickling. Their graves are marked by iron crosses.

Born in Bombay, where her father had been sent by the Greek trading and banking firm of Ralli Brothers of Manchester, into which he had married in 1881, Marietta was the eldest of Alexandros and Julia Pallis's three children. She studied botany at Liverpool and entered Newnham College, Cambridge in 1910. By 1913 she had found a study-area in the reedbeds of the Norfolk Broads, which she compared with those of the Danube Delta. Quickly establishing a reputation as a very private person, an eccentric artist and scholar, she was often seen in jodhpurs, khaki-drill, and pith-helmet, with her companion Phyllis.

Grave of Maria Pallis, Hickling

The Broads

123

TG 424 249

In 1935 she purchased a derelict reed-farm of 32ha at Long Gore and built her studio at a cottage overlooking the marsh in 1936. In 1952 she recruited local labour to dig out her water garden, designed by Jack Thaine. The work on this extraordinary enterprise was completed by 1960.

Marietta Pallis died in Norwich on 30 August 1963 and was buried in the heart of the eagle water gardens with the full rites of the Greek Orthodox Church. The site, maintained by her family, is surrounded by nine ash saplings - one for each of the muses of Greek mythology.

Norwich southern bypass

124 Norwich southern bypass at the Watton Road intersection
TG 165 078 Open

The large scar on the landscape is created by the earthworks for the Norwich southern bypass west of the city at Colney and Bawburgh. Work on the bypass started in 1990 and the road was opened in 1992. It consisted of 23km of dual carriageway from Easton to Postwick and included seven junctions, six of them split-level. In the foreground are the excavations for the junction with the B1108, Norwich-Watton road, with the construction work extending northwards across the valley of the River Yare.

The junction provides for the dual carriageway bypass and slip roads to a flyover with double roundabouts. Adjoining the works is a contractors' site and a garden centre, and the aerial mast in the middle of the photograph is on the site of the now defunct underground emergency regional centre of government. The River Yare meanders across the upper part of the photograph and nearby are lakes created by former sand and gravel workings. Between the river and the lakes gravel is being extracted for the road works from a 'borrow pit' (subsequently to become an additional lake).

This elevated site, lying atop a steep slope overlooking the Yare valley, was also occupied during the remoter past. The Norfolk Archaeological Unit maintained a watching brief on the construction of the entire length of the new road, and a series of pits containing large quantities of Bronze Age pottery was recorded during the earthmoving works for this junction. These discoveries, along with other chance finds of pottery and metalwork, certainly indicate a human presence here in the second millennium BC. Many of the prehistoric living-sites found on the line of the bypass occurred in similar, rather windswept, locations. The remains of cropmark 'ring-ditches', probably indicating the sites of Neolithic or Bronze Age round barrows (23) have also been recorded close by. These mounds may have been clearly visible from the valley bottom in prehistoric times.

The photograph shows the site of another junction under construction on the Norwich southern bypass at Costessey. The road running diagonally across the top of the photo is the (then) A47 Norwich-Dereham Trunk Road, with the roundabout at the access to the Longwater industrial site and gravel workings (now a retail park with Sainsburys and other stores). West of the roadworks (to the left of the picture) is part of the Royal Norfolk Showground. The photograph shows the large area of land needed for a grade-separated intersection. Two roundabouts, a connecting bridge and slip roads are under construction with the excavations for the main dual carriageway running through the centre of the site. The characteristic sand and gravel geology of the area is clearly visible in the picture.

Norwich southern bypass, Costessey

Norwich southern bypass

125

TG 155 106 Open

Military installations

126 Pulham Market airship station

TM 196 836

Pulham air station was commissioned in February 1916 as No. 2 Coastal Airship Station, and was run by the Navy. It remained a base for British airships until they were abandoned. During the Second World War the air station served as a maintenance unit and store for the Royal Air Force, and was finally closed in 1958.

The remains of the bases to be seen in the photograph to centre right are the large concrete bases for the No. 1 and No. 2 sheds which used to house the airships. No. 1 shed was not demolished until 1948, but No. 2 shed was dismantled in 1929 and taken to Cardington to house the new R.100 and R.101 airships. The line of trees to the right of the bases shows where concrete foundations still exist for the massive wind breaks needed to allow the huge airships to be handled on the ground. Immediately to the left of the bases can be seen the silicol plant house for making hydrogen for the airships. Circular stands for the gas holders used to store the gas can just be seen near the lower left hand side of the photograph. In the centre foreground can be seen the concrete base of the earliest small hangar built on the station to house the First World War airships.

The air station was served by a branch line from the nearby Waveney Valley railway line. It terminated near the sheds to the right of the gas holders. Concrete bases for a mooring mast can still be found in the tree clump at top centre of the photograph.

Searchlight installation, Shropham

Military installations

127

TL 972 919

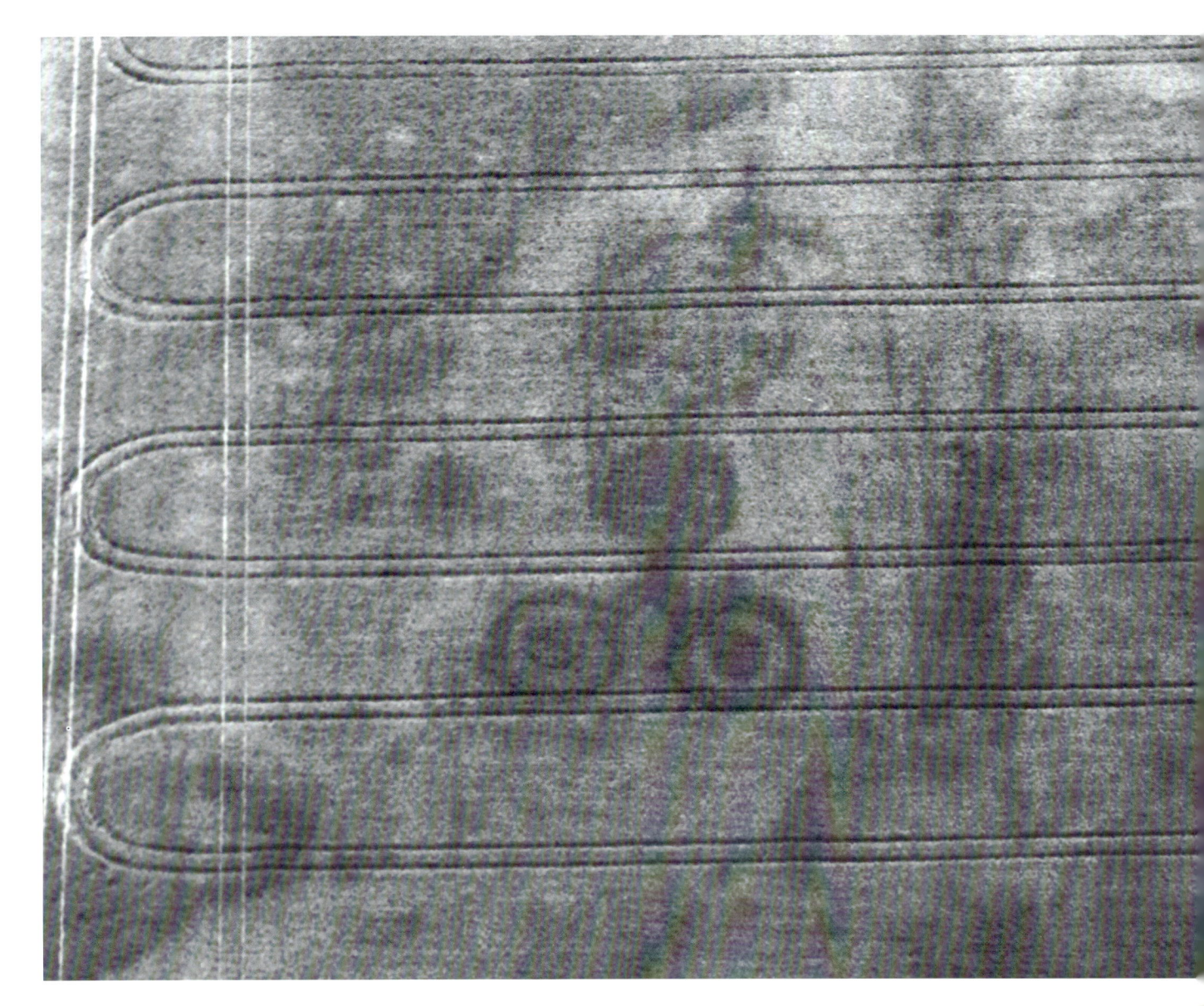

Crop-marks do not always provide proof of ancient habitation. The three linked circles in this photograph of a field about 3km east of the village of Great Hockham, near to the former Snetterton airfield, are all that remain of an anti-aircraft searchlight installation dating from about 1940. Until the middle of the Second World War, almost the entire country was covered with a network of such installations because they were the only way that anti-aircraft guns could detect their targets in the night skies. Searchlights also forced enemy aircraft to fly higher, thus reducing their bombing accuracy.

Each of the three circles shown is about 9m across, and the outer ring marks where a protective earth wall once stood, probably sandbagged, about 1.6m to 1.8m high. The two lower circles, with the better defined 'disc' inside, each held a 0.9m diameter carbon-arc searchlight of several million candlepower intensity, the disc being a concrete hardstanding to provide a stable base. The upper circle was for the predictor or sound locator which guided the searchlight crews to their targets overhead, picking them out for the close attention of the nearby anti-aircraft guns. The lines between the circles were simply pathways for the crews. Wooden huts near the site provided accommodation for these crews and weather protection for the generator powering the searchlights.

As the war progressed, accurate gun-laying radar was developed to guide anti-aircraft weapons to their targets, thereby rendering searchlights unnecessary for this purpose. Such installations became obsolete and were dismantled before the end of the war, rarely leaving much more than the crop-marks you can see in the photograph.

Military installations

128 Mundesley coastal battery

■ N   TG 312 368 Open

This photograph shows a Second World War coastal battery at Mundesley. When Britain was threatened by invasion in 1940 the coasts were quickly fortified. Trenches were dug, obstacles erected, pillboxes built and gun batteries installed. Along the Norfolk coast there were eventually eleven batteries, each armed with two guns, with a further three batteries at Yarmouth. This battery at Mundesley is very typical of the defences of the time, and the best-preserved in the county. It was built in 1941, manned by 197 Battery Royal Artillery and armed with two elderly 6-inch guns which had begun their careers in a First World War battleship. These moderately powerful guns fired a 100-pound (45kg) shell a little over 19km. The guns were fixed to the large octagonal concrete bases and the square steel plates with their rings of bolts for securing the gun mountings can be clearly seen. Originally there would have been a steel frame covered with sandbags to give overhead protection. Magazines for the ammunition and shelters for the crew were located in the buried structure, the concrete roof of which can be seen, running between the two gun positions. The battery was also equipped with two powerful searchlights. The positions for these were sited at the cliff's edge and have long ago fallen over, but the two flat-roofed buildings that housed the diesel generators can be seen a few metres behind the battery. The range finder and battery command post was at the edge of the cliff near where the cars are parked. The battery had an undistinguished war service and as the danger of invasion receded in 1944 it was closed and the troops posted elsewhere. The guns remained until the winter of 1945/46 when they were removed and scrapped.

New airport terminal, Norwich

New impacts on the landscape

TG 215 130 Open

Norwich airport was originally built in 1939 as a base for British bombers but was used by fighters during the Battle of Britain. Later it became the base for American Liberator bombers. After the War it reverted to the Royal Air Force and became a fighter station until it was closed in 1963 (**Vol.1: 125**). The airfield was re-opened, as Norwich Airport, in 1967.

The picture shows the present state of the airfield. The terminal building, opened in 1989, is the white and red building on the edge of the flying field, in the centre of the photograph. The black runway behind it is the original main runway, replaced by the runway just visible in the top left-hand corner. To the right of the new terminal building is the white, new, air freight terminal with the original passenger terminal, of pre-fabs, to the right of that. The five original hangars form a crescent beyond, two being used for aircraft maintenance and three by Anglian Windows. The new white and red hangar to the top of the photograph has been built to house larger aeroplanes. The concrete hardstanding, laid in the 1950s, is beyond it. The triangular concrete tracks each side of the perimeter track near the top left of the photograph are the remains of dispersal points. The bomb dump used to be just beyond the parked aircraft at the top of the picture.

The other buildings are industrial units forming the Airport Industrial Estate. Old Catton is in the top right-hand corner, and the Stakis Hotel is the large red complex in the foreground. The grid-like rectangle beside the terminal is the passenger car park. Norwich Airport is a successful venture, with passenger, freight and private plane services and a thriving aircraft repair and repainting business.

New impacts on the landscape
130 King's Lynn power station

TF 608 177

The King's Lynn power station is located on the south side of the town, within an 8ha site owned by Eastern Generation. The station is operated by Anglian Power Generators Ltd, a wholly-owned subsidiary of Eastern Generation. The Great Ouse River is to the west and to the north is the site of the old sugar beet factory and Lynn's Speedway Stadium.

Construction started in October 1994 and since August 1996 the station has been generating electricity. The site was handed over by the German contractor, Siemens, in December 1997.

The 340 mega watts combined cycle gas turbine (CCGT) power station is designed to achieve high thermal efficiency as well as generating power in an environmentally friendly way. Using gas supplied via British Gas Transco's main pipeline from the Bacton terminal, a gas turbine, similar to a jet engine, is fuelled. The exhaust heat is then used to heat water to produce steam that in turn runs the steam turbine. Both the gas and steam turbine drive the same single generator, with a clutch between the generator and steam turbine.

At full capacity, the station can generate enough electricity to power three towns the size of King's Lynn. The output of the station varies quite widely at different temperatures, being lower at high temperatures and higher at low temperatures - very convenient when the National Grid needs peak load on a bleak winter's day! The generated electricity is distributed to customers via the Eastern Electricity distribution network.

The Swaffham EcoTech Centre

New impacts on the landscape

TF 816 099 Open

EcoTech is intended to raise awareness about the wonders of our environment. It introduces sustainable, hi-tec ideas to encourage us to care more for the world in which we live. The project is a unique partnership which has won £2m from the European Regional Challenge Fund and £1m from the Rural Development Commissions' Rural Challenge competitions.

Awareness of the environment has been crucial to the design of EcoTech. It uses the latest environmentally friendly technology and the largest volume of timber of any structure in the region. Over 225 cubic metres of Norwegian Spruce weighing 125 tonnes have been used for the timber-framed structure. EcoTech maximises solar energy. The high level of glazing on the sloping southern side will transmit heat from the sun deep into the building, acting as a heat store. The northern side is highly insulated to reduce heat loss and will keep the building warm even in winter. Extra heating will use a biomass system: the burning of locally grown, sustainable, fast-growing wood, usually willow, to provide energy.

The EcoTech centre includes a business suite. This offers a full range of office services, support and training specially targetted at emerging hi-tech businesses. Conference and seminar facilities are also available and links are being made with Cambridge Science Park, Norwich Research Park and the University of East Anglia. The Discovery Centre Visitor Attraction will be an enjoyable, fun way to find out about the environment and how to safeguard it. Original, interactive hands-on displays and demonstrations, video images, CD rom music, sounds and graphics will be used.

The EcoTech Organic Garden Group is a community-based group, developing an organic and wildlife show garden on a 0.4ha site within the grounds of EcoTech. The group's goals include promoting organic fruit and vegetable husbandry, hedge laying and hurdle making, rainwater collection and irrigation, and gardening for the disabled.

New impacts on the landscape
132 Welmore Lake sluice, Welney

TL 570 985

The Ouse Washes form a vital component of the flood defences of the Middle and South Levels of the Cambridgeshire fens, providing flood storage and conveyance when the normal channels are at full capacity. A strategic study of the system was completed in 1995 by the Environment Agency which recommended that summer flooding should be better controlled and that the structures contained within the Washes be improved.

One of those structures is Welmore Lake Sluice. It is located 20km south of King's Lynn. It has a dual function in holding back tidal waters from entering the Ouse Washes and also allowing flood waters to rejoin the river system once the flood has passed by. Such an event occurred during Easter 1998 and the above picture illustrates the extensive storage capacity of the Washes.

Work on reconstructing the sluice commenced in July 1997 and has advanced to the point at which the concrete piers can be seen emerging from the steel circular cofferdam. The new structure is 50% bigger than the old one and will include three vertical steel gates to control the upstream water levels. The steel cofferdam allows construction to take place in the dry and will be removed once the new gates have been installed. It is due to be completed in July 1999 at an estimated cost of £5.2m.

New impacts on the landscape
Barnham Broom Hotel and golf course
133
TG 088 088 Open

Set in 100ha of Norfolk countryside along the banks of the River Yare, Barnham Broom Hotel, golf, conference and leisure complex has grown to become one of the premier golf resorts in the country. The fifty-three bedroom hotel with two eighteen-hole golf courses and the other facilities provides all the amenities for the business and leisure market.

The buildings at the bottom right of the photograph are Timeshare and Holiday Property Bond apartments. Above them is the leisure centre, then the hotel, and finally, at the top of the photograph, are the conference centre and tennis courts. To the right is the Valley Course, which was built on marshland and designed by Frank Pennink in 1977. The Hill Course, which is not visible in the picture, was designed by Donald Steele and opened in 1989.

Within the hotel is Flints Restaurant together with the Valley Bar which overlooks the golf course. In addition the Sports Buttery Bar is open all day for light meals.

The leisure centre comprises an indoor heated swimming pool, sauna and steam room, gymnasium, solarium, four squash courts and three tennis courts. A hairdressing and beauty salon is also available.

New impacts on the landscape
134 West Somerton wind farm

TG 475 191

The ten towers of the wind farm at West Somerton are set within a very typical area of rural east Norfolk. Looking almost north-west, West Somerton church is on the right and above and to the west of that is the village at the head of its dyke leading from the River Thurne. Martham Broad lies above the wood to the left of the village, and beyond that can just be seen Heigham Sound at the southern end of Hickling Broad. The large arable fields with few hedges and some surviving hedge-line trees are characteristic of much of arable Norfolk, where the few farm animals are housed in yards or barns. The picture was taken in August, so cereal crops are harvested or just about to be cut, whilst the very dark green fields are in sugar beet with poor patches due to the dry summer of 1994.

The wind farm, so far the only one in Norfolk, is sited near the coast to take advantage of the stronger and more persistent winds. Each unit is on a tower 30m high, and the diameter of the blades is 27m. The total capacity of all ten turbines is 2.25 mega watts, and the output from this small wind farm is enough to provide about 5% of the power for the Borough of Great Yarmouth. With the threat of global warming, increasing power from non-fossil supplies is very necessary, and currently power companies have an obligation to develop alternatives such as wind power. The visual impact of these generators limits the areas where planners find them acceptable, though many people find the West Somerton group attractive.

Castoro 10 pipelaying vessel

The North Sea

TG 34 38

The pipeline construction and trenching vessel *Castoro 10* is seen here operating on the Shell Sole Pit Project in offshore waters in 1990. The project included the installation and trenching of 73km of 24-inch (0.6m) gas pipeline from Bacton to Clipper platform, and 27km of 16-inch (0.4m) gas pipeline from Clipper platform to Barque platform.

The vessel is owned and operated by European Marine Contractors Ltd and carries highly specialised equipment to enable it to construct continuous rigid steel pipelines and then lower them into a seabed trench. The photograph shows the vessel in pipeline trenching mode. Powerful pumping equipment below deck delivers high pressure water to a subsea trenching machine which is lowered over the pipeline from a storage area below the vessel helideck. This trenching machine uses the high pressure water and suction to cut the trench in the seabed for the pipeline to rest in. The function of a trench is to provide the pipeline with protection and stability.

As well as pipelaying and pipe trenching, the *Castoro 10* is home to up to 168 crew members. On board there is a hospital, a galley, and a cinema. A supply vessel can be seen alongside bringing food and provisions for the crew.

Acknowledgements

All the photographs in this second volume were taken by Derek Edwards, Air Photography Officer for the Field Archaeology Division of the Norfolk Museums Service, except for nos. 1 (David Wicks, Norfolk Museums Service), 80, 101, 102, 103 and 104, which have been generously provided as follows:

Aerial Archaeology Publications (103)

The Swain Collection, purchased for the Norfolk Air Photographs Library with the aid of the Science Museum PRISM Grant Fund, (102 and 104)

Royal Air Force (80)

Royal Flying Corps, courtesy of Mrs R. Young (101)

The following authors have very kindly written captions, and the editor wishes to express his sincere thanks to them:

David Adshead, 68, 71
Diane Akers, 86
Trevor Ashwin, 18, 19, 20, 21, 22, 23, 24, 25, 124
Brian Ayers, 103, 104, 105, 106, 107, 108
John Ayton, 124, 125
Michael Barrett, 94
Christopher Barringer, 8, 43, 63, 64, 69, 87, 88, 89, 90, 98, 99, 100
Neil Batcock, 51
Andrew Beane, 130
Philippa Beardmore, 131
Michael Begley, 14, 54
Keith Clayton, 2, 3, 4, 6, 9, 10, 11, 12, 13, 17, 134
Donna Clubb, 133
Martin Collier, 82, 83, 84
Kevin Cooper, 135
Brian Cushion, 49, 57, 65, 66
John Davies, 26, 35, 36

Alan Davison, 39, 40, 41, 42, 46, 49, 50, 52, 57, 58, 59, 60, 61
Jim Durrant, 110
Derek Edwards, 1, 101, 102, 123
Jane Everett, 56
Annie Fisher, 109
David Gurney, 28, 29, 30, 31, 32, 33, 34, 37, 38
Henry Head, 85
Stephen Heywood, 55
Christine Hiskey, 75
Kevin Hitchcock, 91
Jonathan Hooton, 5, 7
James Keith, 81
Peter Kent, 128
Reg Land, 115, 118
Alan Mackley, 76, 77, 78
Bob Malster, 122
Derek and Mary Manning, 97, 112, 113, 114, 126, 129
Ronald Pestell, 53
Kevan Platt, 111
Simon Purcell, 127
Paul Richards, 95, 96
Robert Rickett, 47
Paul Rutledge, 62, 93
Diana Shipp, 116, 117, 119, 120, 121
Hassell Smith, 70
Melissa Tembe, 132
Susanna Wade Martins, 79, 80
Peter Wade-Martins, 27, 67
Tom Williamson, 15, 16, 48, 72
David Yaxley, 44, 73, 74, 92
Susan Yaxley, 45

Norfolk Museums Service gratefully acknowledges the grant aid and administrative support given by the Royal Commission on the Historical Monuments of England, which has contributed to the success of the Norfolk Museums Service aerial reconnaissance programme.

Dates and sources of the photographs

In the following catalogue, the photographs are listed in the order in which they appear in the book. The first entry is the figure number; the second entry is the date of the photograph; the third entry is the copyright owner; the fourth entry is the copyright holder's reference number. All the photographs were taken by Derek A. Edwards, except where otherwise indicated.

Abbreviations used
AAP Photograph from the H. Frederick Low Collection, Aerial Archaeology Publications, Lansdown House, Breton Close, Toftwood, Dereham, Norfolk NR19 1JH.
NAPL Norfolk Aerial Photography Library, Union House, Gressenhall, Dereham, Norfolk NR20 4DR
NAPL/PRISM Photograph from the Swain Collection, Norfolk Aerial Photography Library, courtesy of the Science Museum PRISM Grant Fund), Union House, Gressenhall, Dereham, Norfolk NR20 4DR
RAF Royal Air Force
RFC Royal Flying Corps, courtesy of Mrs R.Young

Illustrations
Frontispiece 06 Jul 94 NAPL TG4015/S/Slide
1   13 Mar 91 NAPL FJS1 (Photo by David Wicks)
2   15 Aug 95 NAPL TG4228/A/HHJ4
3   21 Feb 96 NAPL TG3830/AB/HFH5
4   10 Jul 86 NAPL TG1643/A/DDF9
5   12 Jul 93 NAPL TG0244/T/HFX23
6   21 Feb 96 NAPL TG0844/N/HFF12
7   22 Sep 87 NAPL TG0444/E/DFJ6
8   10 Jul 86 NAPL TF9143/P/DDG5
9   26 Jun 89 NAPL TF9246/B/DSF2
10 07 May 86 NAPL TF7946/R/DES9
11 19 Jun 90 NAPL TF6742/K
12 18 Jul 81 NAPL TF7317/B/Slide
13 12 Jul 93 NAPL TG0143/H/HFX20
14 26 Jul 88 NAPL TF5114/F/DJR10
15 11 Jul 86 NAPL TG4509/A/DDM11
16 30 Jun 86 NAPL TG4604/AF/DAJ11
17 27 Jul 86 NAPL TL9087/D/DEB12
18 15 Jul 96 NAPL TG2326/P/HJV7
19 09 Jun 92 NAPL TG2521/C/GLQ4
20 09 Jul 92 NAPL TG2035/X/GLS6
21 25 Jun 96 NAPL TG2406/AFH/HKT37
22 14 Jun 96 NAPL TG2305/AGG/HMY14
23 21 Feb 89 NAPL TF7627/T/DGG4
24 14 Jun 74 NAPL TG2204/W/AAW20
25 05 Apr 90 NAPL TG2204/ACU/DZN9
26 15 Apr 83 NAPL TF7513/E/AST19
27 04 Jul 89 NAPL TM1996/P/DPN9
28 05 Jul 89 NAPL TF6638/R/DMA4
29 26 Jun 89 NAPL TF9923/AJ/DSD4
30 26 Jun 96 NAPL HYB8
31 12 Jul 89 NAPL TL7587/ACB/DMJ14
32 22 Jul 96 NAPL TF8800/AQ/HMZ24
33 22 Jul 96 NAPL TF8800/AJ/HJX26
34 16 Jun 89 NAPL TG0119/ADA/DJB11
35 14 Jun 96 NAPL TG2303/ANQ/HMY9
36 15 Jun 89 NAPL TG2303/AMD/DHW9
37 15 Jun 89 NAPL TG2303/AET/SLIDE
38 29 Jun 93 NAPL TG0802/AG/HAE11
39 10 Dec 91 NAPL TF6511/AA/EV8
40 26 Mar 85 NAPL TM2689/D/AYG17
41 10 Dec 91 NAPL TF6616/T/LZ5
42 29 Jun 95 NAPL TF9119/ADN/HBZ8
43 10 Dec 91 NAPL TF8115/AEM/Z2
44 29 Jul 83 NAPL TG5012/S/ATQ21
45 10 Dec 91 NAPL TF8114/ADC/Z8
46 27 Jul 86 NAPL TL8683/AV/DCQ19
47 01 Aug 90 NAPL TF9336/AY/GEM9
48 30 Jun 89 NAPL TG3815/AS/DLH5
49 09 Feb 84 NAPL TF7009/V/ATZ29
50 26 Jun 89 NAPL TF6809/AF/DJY7
51 29 Jun 92 NAPL TF8228/A/GKS4
52 29 Jun 92 NAPL TF8429/ACL/GKS11
53 29 Apr 91 NAPL TG4128/D/GGM4
54 26 Jul 88 NAPL TF5716/M/DJQ10
55 27 Apr 84 NAPL TM3898/D/AWY17
56 30 Jun 89 NAPL TG122/H/DQU9
57 23 Feb 89 NAPL TL6298/Y/DGN4
58 05 Feb 84 NAPL TG2504/X/ATU4
59 09 Feb 84 NAPL TF8220/L/AUG25
60 08 Jul 76 NAPL TF7119/D/AFY10
61 25 Feb 76 NAPL TF8836/T/AEB4
62 05 Feb 84 NAPL TM0990/C/ATS5
63 15 Jul 86 NAPL TF9520/D/DDQ7
64 29 Jun 76 NAPL TG0813/A/AFB5
65 23 Feb 89 NAPL TL6197/A/DGN11
66 23 Feb 89 NAPL TF6605/B/DGQ2
67 15 Jul 86 NAPL TF6617/F/DDR15
68 22 Jul 97 NAPL TF7401/ABR/HPY11
69 10 Jul 85 NAPL TF6941/Q/AYY24
70 10 Jul 85 NAPL TF9742/H/AZA13
71 29 Jul 86 NAPL TG1728/Z/DCS16
72 26 Jun 89 NAPL TF8220/Y/DKG5
73 26 Jun 89 NAPL TF7928/AC/DKG10
74 22 Jul 97 NAPL TF7828/Q/HPZ9
75 10 Jul 86 NAPL TF8842/N/DDG14
76 05 Apr 90 NAPL TG2202/P/DZP14
77 27 Jul 95 NAPL TG2202/Z/HEF9
78 22 Sep 86 NAPL TF6928/E/DFH7
79 03 Mar 86 NAPL TF8633/C/AZN14
80 30 Mar 46 RAF 3G/TUD/UK100 Part V, Frames 5364 & 5366 [NAPL Copy-negs ref: FSG11 and FSG13] (Photo Royal Air Force)
81 15 Aug 95 NAPL TF9917/G/HHG28
82 02 Aug 95 NAPL TG3022/C/HQZ12
83 18 Aug 86 NAPL TG0624/D/DEH9
84 18 Aug 86 NAPL TG1025/K/DEF10
85 10 Jul 86 NAPL TF6837/L/DDH12

145

86 01 Jul 87 NAPL TG1510/G/DEX7
87 29 Jun 95 NAPL TG1127/AN/HEC9
88 17 Jul 84 NAPL TG3026/A
89 04 Oct 91 NAPL TM0495/Q/GJE6
90 30 Jun 89 NAPL TG1927/Q/DQV11
91 08 Jul 88 NAPL TF6103/H/DVG3
92 26 Apr 84 NAPL TF9129/K/AWD3
93 27 Jul 95 NAPL TG5207/ABP/HEZ1
94 18 Jul 88 NAPL TG0738/K/DWC13
95 11 Sep 87 NAPL TF6119/J/DFG2
96 11 Sep 87 NAPL TF6120/AF/DFG6
97 17 Aug 88 NAPL TG2830/J/DTV13
98 24 Jun 98 NAPL TF8108/Q/HTP5
99 10 Jul 96 NAPL TF9100/B/HQY5
100 23 Sep 87 NAPL TG1001/ABS/DQL10
101 17 May 17 MoD NAPL Copyneg RFC-036
(Photo Royal Flying Corps, Courtesy Mrs R. Young)
102 c.1921 NAPL/PRISM Swain Collection 357
(Photo the late George Ernest Swain)
103 c.1938 AAP LOW-103 (Photo the late H. Frederick Low)
104 c.1951 NAPL/PRISM Swain Collection P.9.1.
(Photo the late George Ernest Swain)
105 05 Aug 94 NAPL TG2208/ACJ/GZH5
106 15 Jun 89 NAPL TG2308/BAN/DHY7
107 18 May 92 NAPL TG2308/AVX/GJK12
108 27 Jul 94 NAPL TG2308/BDQ/GZF9
109 15 Oct 93 NAPL TG2011/J/HGJ22
110 02 Aug 95 NAPL TG1907/AR/HHQ21
111 02 Aug 95 NAPL TG2407/ABP/HHR18
112 23 Sep 87 NAPL TG1002/D/DQL8
113 30 Jun 89 NAPL TG1117/N/DQT3
114 27 Jul 95 NAPL TG5305/C/HEG21
115 12 Jul 90 NAPL TG4120/E/GDD5
116 11 Jul 86 NAPL TG4513/A/DDM15
117 21 Aug 90 NAPL TG4111/G/GFJ2
118 21 Aug 90 NAPL TG3813/E/GFJ4
119 27 Nov 95 NAPL TG3522/E/HFG1
120 30 Jun 86 NAPL TG3416/V/DAM5
121 02 Aug 95 NAPL TG3116/M/HEP23
122 08 Apr 97 NAPL TG4001/H/HPM1
123 12 Jul 90 NAPL TG4224/A/GDE2
124 12 Jun 91 NAPL TG1607/F/GGR14
125 04 Oct 91 NAPL TG1510/AJ/Slide
126 06 Aug 93 NAPL TM1983/F/GST13
127 15 Jun 89 NAPL TL9791/K/DHN11
128 31 Jul 84 NAPL TG3136/D/AXX4
129 15 Aug 95 NAPL TG2113/G/HGW3
130 08 May 98 NAPL TF6017/F/HSX14
131 24 Jun 98 NAPL TF8109/N/HTP2
132 08 May 98 NAPL TL5798/B/HSX1
133 19 Jun 95 NAPL TG0808/Z/HBT18
134 05 Aug 94 NAPL TF4719/H/Slide
135 11 Jul 89 NAPL TG3438/D/DSG11

Suggestions for further reading

Norfolk

Ayers, B. (1994) *The English Heritage Book of Norwich*, London, Batsford

Margeson, S., Seillier, F. & Rogerson, A. (1994) *The Normans in Norfolk*, Norwich, Norfolk Museums Service

Margeson, S., Ayers, B. & Heywood, S. [eds] (1996) *A Festival of Norfolk Archaeology,* Norwich, Norfolk & Norwich Archaeological Society

Martins, S.W. (1988) *Norfolk, A Changing Countryside*, Chichester, Phillimore

Martins, S.W. (1997) *A History of Norfolk*, (2nd Edition) Chichester, Phillimore

Meeres, F. (1998) *A History of Norwich*, Chichester, Phillimore

Wade-Martins, P. [ed.] (1993) *Historical Atlas of Norfolk*, Norwich, Norfolk Museums Service

Williamson, T. (1993) *The Origins of Norfolk*, Manchester, Manchester University Press

Williamson, T. (1997) *The Norfolk Broads, a Landscape History*, Manchester, Manchester University Press

Aerial Photography

Allen Brown, R. (1989) *Castles from the Air*, Cambridge, Cambridge University Press

Bayliss-Smith, T & Owens, S. [eds] (1990) *Britain's Changing Environment from the Air*, Cambridge, Cambridge University Press

Burton, N. (1989) *English Heritage from the Air*, London, Sidgwick & Jackson

Combe Books (1991) *England from the Air*, London, Tiger Books

Darvill, T. (1996) *Prehistoric Britain from the Air*, Cambridge, Cambridge University Press

Gardiner, L. (1989) *The Changing Face of Britain - from the Air*, Michael Joseph, London

Glasscock, R. (1992) *Historic Landscapes of Britain from the Air*, Cambridge, Cambridge University Press

Hawkes, J. & Struthers, J. (1993) *Britain from the Air*, London, Ebury Press

Start, D. (1993) *Lincolnshire from the Air*, Sleaford, Heritage Lincolnshire

Strachan, D. (1998) *Essex from the Air*, Chelmsford, Essex County Council

Tinniswood, A. & Hawkes, J. (1994) *Country Houses from the Air*, London, Weidenfeld & Nicolson

Unichrome Books (1996) *Over Historical England*, Bath, Unichrome

Wade-Martins, P. [ed.] (1997) *Norfolk from the Air 1* [Vol. 1, 2nd Edition] Norwich, Norfolk Museums Service

Index of place names

This index refers by picture number to places illustrated or mentioned in the text. Bold figures refer to the titles of the photographs; other figures indicate a text reference.

Acle 117, 122
   Bridge **117**, 116
Anmer 74
Ant, the 119
Arminghall **21**, 19, 22, 24/5
Attleborough **89**
   Church of St Mary 89
   Connaught Road 89
   Queen's Square 89
   Royal Hotel 89
Aylsham **90**, 87
   Church of St. Michael 90
   Market Place 90
   Millgate 90
   Red Lion Street 90
   Town Hall 90
   White Hart Street 90

Babingley 65
Bacton 130, 135
Barnham Broom Hotel **133**
Barningham Hall 76
Barton 119
   Broad 119
   Turf **119**
Barton Bendish 32
Bath, Wilts 56
Bawburgh 124
Bawdeswell 63, 90
Bintree **29**
Bishop's Lynn 95
Bixley **21**, 58
   Hall 58
Blackwater, the 33/34
Blakeney **5**, 13
   Bob Hall's Sands **9**
   Esker **13**
   Holgate Way 5
   Mariner's Hill 5
   Point 5, **6**, 9
Blickling Hall **71**
Bombay, India 123
Booton **56**
   Church of St Michael 56
Brancaster **10**, 11
   Harbour 10
Breckland 17, 99
   Fenmere 17
   Langmere 17
   Ringmere 17
Breydon Water **16**, 15
Brisley Green **63**
   Panford Beck 63
Broadland 16, 48
Broads, the 2, 115, 116, 117, 118, 120, 123
   Barton Broad 119
   Cockshoot Broad 120

Filby Broad 116
Hickling Broad 134
Martham Broad 134
Muck Fleet 116
Ormesby Broad 116
Ormesby Little Broad 116
Trinity Broads 116
Upton Broad 118
Wroxham Broad 121
Bromholme Priory 90
Buckenham 122
Bure, the 19, 48, 90, 116, 118, 121, 122
Bungay, Suffolk 58
Burgh-next-Aylsham 56
Burgh St Margaret 116
Burnham Overy Staithe 10

Caister **44**
   Castle 44
   Hall 44
   Pickerell's Fleet 44
Caistor St Edmund 22, 24/25, 35, 36, 37, 21, 38, 99
   Harford Farm 24/5
Caley Mill Lavender Farm **85**
California, Norfolk 116
Cambridge 91, 123
   Science Park 131
Canada 12
Castle Acre **43**, 45, 80
   Castle **43**
   Church of St James 43
   Priory **45**
   Town 43
Cawston 32, 87
Cley-next-the-Sea **7**, 5, 6
   Beau Rivage 7
   Holfleete 7
   Milsteade 7
Cluny Abbey, Burgundy 45
Coddenham, Suffolk 36
Coldham Hall 122
Colney 124
Coltishall **19**
Costessey **86**, **125**
   Longwater Industrial Estate 125
   Royal Norfolk Showground 125
Coxford Priory **51**, **52**
Crete 7
Cromer 3, **4**, 90
   Ridge 4
Crownthope 99

Danube Delta 123
Darrow Green 40
Denton 40
   Darrow (Dearhaugh) Wood 40
Denver 99
Dereham 99, 100, 125
Diss 89
Downham Market **91**
   Bridge Street 91

   Church 91
   Courthouse 91
   High Street 91
   Priory 91
   Town Hall 91
   Workhouse 91
Dunham 42
Dunston Hall **76**, **77**

Easton 124
East Rudham **51**, **52**
East Walton 12
   Common 12
   Pingos 12
Eccles **53**, 2
   Church 53

Fakenham **92**
   Corn Hall 92
   Crown Inn 92
   Red Lion Inn 92
   Tunn Street 92
Fen Causeway 99
Fenland 12, 57
Fenmore 17
Fens, the 26, 91, 99
Filby 116
   Broad **116**
Flitcham 74
Fring 85
Fritton 55

Gayton **60**
   West Hall Bushey Close 60
   West Hall Close 60
   West Hall Manor 60
Gillingham 122
Glandford 7, 13
Glasgow 103-5
Glaven, the 7, 13
Great Hockham 127
Great Ouse, the 14, 91, 96, 130
Great Yarmouth **93**, **114**, 5, 8, 15, 116, 117, 122, 128, 134
   Blind Middlegate 93
   Church of St Nicholas 93
   Howard Street 93
   King Street 93
   Market Gates 93
   Market Place 93
   Power Station 114
   Priory 93
   South Denes 114

Hales 55
Halvergate Marshes **15**, 17
   'Acle Straight' 15
   Stacey Arms Mill 15
Hanworth **20**, 18
Happisburgh **3**
   Beach Road 3
Harpley **23**, 74
Heacham **28**, 85
Heckingham 55
   Church 55

Heigham Sound 134
Hemsby 116
Heydon **87**
   Common 87
   Hall 76
Hickling **123**
   Broad **115**, 134
   Long Gore Marsh 123
Hilgay **57**, **66**, 65
   Fen 57
   Lodge Farm 66
Hockering **64**
   Home Pastures 64
   Park 64
   Park Farm 64
Hockwold-cum-Wilton **31**
Hoe **81**
Holkham 26, 80
   Bay 10, 11
   Estate 8, 61, 79
   Hall **75**
   Marshes 8
Holme-next-the-Sea 11
   Gore Point 11
Holt **94**, 5, 87
   Bull Street 94
   Corn Hall 94
   Feathers Hotel 94
   Fish Hill 94
   Gresham's School 94
   High Street 94
   Magistrates Court 94
   Market 94
   Old School House 94
   Quaker Chapel 94
   Shire Hall 94
Honingham 64
Horning 48, **120**, 122
   Ferry Inn 120
   St Benet's Abbey 48
   The Chequers 48
Horsey 2
Horsford 39
Horstead with Stanninghall 32
Houghton 74
   Hall **73**, 74, 71
   New Houghton 74
Hoveton 121
How Hill 119
Hunstanton 11
   Hall **69**
   Park 11
   St Edmund's Point 11

Iceland 7
Icknield Way 26
Ireland 15
Islington **54**
   Church 54
   Hall 54

King's Lynn **95**, **96**, 8, 12, 14, 39, 60, 69, 91, 98, 117, 132
   Bishop's Lynn 95
   Church of St Margaret 95
   Common Staithe 96

Corn Exchange 96
Gaywood 95, 96
Guildhall of St George 96
King Street 96
Nelson Street 95
'Newland' 96
Power Station **130**
Purfleet 96
St Margaret's House 95
St Nicholas Chapel 96
Saturday Market Place **95**, 96
South Quay 95
Town Hall 95
Trinity Guildhall 95
Tuesday Market Place **96**
Queen Street 95

Langmere 17
Lenwade **113**
  Concrete Works **113**
Lessingham **53**
Lichfield, Staffs 56
Litcham 42, 63
Lewes Castle, Sussex 43
Little Walsingham **47**
  Market Place 47
  Walsingham Way 47
Liverpool 123
London 8, 47, 89

Marham **49**
  Abbey **49**
Marshland 14, 54
Middleton **41**
  Castle Hall 41
  Mount 41
  Tower End 41
  Towers **67**
Mileham **42**
  Burghwood Manor 42
  Burwood Hall 42
  Castle 42
Morston 13
Mundesley **128**, 56

Nar, the 26, 39, 43, 45, 80
Narborough 26, 12, 27
Nene, the 14
New Buckenham **62**
  Common **62**
  Spittlemere 62
New Hunstanton 11, 69
Newton Church 80
Nogdam End, Norton Subcourse 122
Normandy 58
North Creake 92
North Elmham 63
  Burgrave Wood 63
North Walsham **97**, 88, 90
  Church of St Nicholas 97
  Market Street 97
Norway 10
Norwich **101**, **102**, **103-5**, **106-8**, **109**, **110**, **111**, 15, 16, 46, 58, 76, 88, 89, 90, 98, 110, 122, 124
  Airport terminal **129**
  Anglia TV 106-8
  Back of the Inns 106-8
  Barclays Bank 106-8
  Barn Road 101

Ber Street 106-8
Bethel Hospital 103-5
Britannia Barracks 101
C&A building 103-5
Carrow Road **111**
Castle 101, 106-8
Castle Fee 106-8
Castle Gardens 106-8
Castle Mall **106-8**
Castle Meadow 106-8
Castle Street 106-8
Cathedral 54, 101
Cattle Market **106-8**
City Hall **103-5**, 102
City Station 101
Clover Leaf Cafe 103-5
Duke's Palace 106-8
Farmers' Avenue 106-8
Fire Station 103-5
Gentleman's Walk 102
Graham's Court 102
Grand Opera House 103-5
Great Cockey, the 102, 106-8
Guildhall 102
Hay Hill 103-5
Haymarket 102
Hippodrome 103-5
Library 103-5
London Street 106-8
'Low Court' 102
Mancroft 102
Mancroft Octagon 103-5
Market Place **102**, **203-5**
Market Street 102
Market Tollhouse 102
Memorial Gardens 103-5
Mousehold Aerodrome 101
Mousehold Heath 101
Mousehold Lane 101
New Star Inn 103-5
Police Station 102
Raven Public House 103-5
Research Park **131**
Royal Hotel 106-8
Sir Garnet Wolseley Public House 103-5
St. Giles Street 102, 103-5
St. Peter Mancroft Church 102, 103-5
St. Peter's Street 102, 103-5
Shirehall 106-8
Southern bypass **124**, **125**, 24/5
Sport Village **109**
Thorpe Station 101
Timberhill 106-8
University of East Anglia **110**
Victoria Gardens 101
Victoria Station 101
Worsted Seld 102
Wounded Hart Lane 102

Old Buckenham 40
Old Catton 129
Old Hunstanton **69**, 11
  Church of St Mary 69
Ormesby Broad **116**
Ouse Washes, 132
Oxburgh Hall **68**, 67
Oxnead 76

Pakenham, Suffolk 36
Peddars Way 33/34
Postwick 124
Pulham Market 126

Raynham Hall 70
Reedham **16**, **122**
  Berney Arms Mill 16
Reepham 87
Ringmere 17
Rougham **59**, **72**
  Hall 72
  Hildemere 59
  Lynn Way 59
  Massingham Gate 59
  Overgate 59
  Park 72
Roughton 19
Royal Norfolk Showground 125

Saham Toney **32**, **33**, **34**
  Woodcock Hall 32/33
St Benet's Abbey, Horning **48**, 88
  Cow Holm 48
Salle **84**, 87
Salthouse **6**, 3, 7
Sandringham House **78**
Scolt Head **10**
  Island 11
Scotland 10, 15
Scratby 116
Sea Palling **2**
Severn Valley, Gloucs 17
Sheringham **4**
Shouldham **50**
  Abbey Farm 50
  Priory 50
Shropham **127**
Snetterton **127**
Snettisham **85**
South Creake **61**, **79**, 26, 92
  Leicester Square Farm **79**
Spixworth 32
Stiffkey
  Hall **70**
  Bridge Street
Stokesby 116, 122
Stonehenge (Wilts) 21
Stradsett **65**
  Park **65**
Surlingham 122
Sutton Bridge 14
Swaffham **30**, **98**, 43, 91
  Assembly Rooms 98
  Church of St Peter and St Paul 98
  Corn Hall 98
  EcoTech Centre **131**
  Hammonds School 98
  Town Hall 98
Swanton Morley **1**, **34**

Tas, the 22, 24/5, 35, 36
Tasburgh **27**, 26
  Church 27
Temple Balsall, West Midlands 56
Themelthorpe **83**
Thetford **46**, 26, 98, 99
Thompson Common 12
Thornham 11, 29
Thurne, the *Frontispiece*, 134
Thurne *Frontispiece*

Tibenham 62
Tiffey, the 100
Tilney All Saints **54**
Titchwell 11
Trunch 56
Tud, the 64
Tunstead **82**
Tuttington **18**

University of East Anglia **110**, 131
Upton Broad **118**

Venta Icenorum 24/5, 35, 37

Walpole **14**
  Highway 14
  St Peter 14
Warham **8**, **27**, **29**, 70
  Bridge Street 70
  St. Mary 26
Wash, the 11
Waterden **61**
Watton **99**, 89, 124
  Back Street 99
  Brook 33/34
  Church of St Mary 99
  High Street 99
  Market 99
Waveney Valley 126
Weavers' Way 117
Wells-next-the-Sea **8**, **9**
  Beach 9
  Church of St Nicholas 8
  Harbour 9, 10
Welmore Lake **132**
Welney **132**
Wensum, the 63, 101, 102, 106-8
Westminster, London 56
Weston Longville **113**
West Runton 4
West Somerton **134**
  Church 134
West Walton 54
Whitlingham 16, 122
Wicklewood **38**, **37**
Wighton 29
Wiltshire 18
Wisbech 14, 91
Wissey, the 99
Wiveton Down 13
Wood Dalling 87
Wormegay **39**
Worstead **88**
  Church 88
  Church Plain 88
  Manor House 88
  Seld 102
Wretham Heath **17**
  Nature Reserve 17
Wroxham Broad **121**
  Hudson's Bay 121
Wymondham **100**, **112**, 99
  Abbey 100
  Brush Factory **112**
  Market Place 100

Yare, the 16, 22, 24/5, 122, 124, 133